People Talk

Norma has made the fundamentals of small business legal issues easy to understand and easy to read. Her book is concise yet complete. I strongly recommend this book as a "must read" for all start-ups and small businesses with an ambition to grow. It is ideal to keep as a great reference source.
 — Steve McCrillis, *FA, MBC, The Biz-Easy Network*

Things Go Wrong is the book I needed when I started my businesses and the one I will reference from now on. It breaks everything down so anyone can understand it while guiding you through every step and question you will have in starting a business.
 — Dr. Ila Foster, *Graceful Hands Chiropractic &*
 Wellness Center

Excellent job of clearly laying out how to start a business and then reminding us all that it is not all about dollars and cents afterwards. Growth and the bottom line can be great, but ignoring HR and general risk management for your business can sink it as quickly as the Titanic. Very well done!
 — Tom Broughton, *TRJ Consulting, LLC*

The most well-written, comprehensive books on business compliance that I have ever read. Norma makes this complex topic easy and fun.
 — Skip Williams, *Biz Easy Network*

THINGS GO
WRONG

Legal Minefields that
Business Owners Hate
But Have to Deal With

NORMA SHIRK

SHIRK BUSINESS BOOKS

Shirk Business Books may be purchased for educational, business or sales promotional use.
For information please write: Norma Shirk, CCRA Press,
P O Box 295, Hermitage, Tennessee 37076
or visit www.complianceriskadvisor.com

Production and creative provided by Epiphany Creative Services LLC
Cover and book design by Jonathan Gullery

Library of Congress Control Number: 2023920198

Library of Congress Cataloging-in-Publication Data:
FIRST EDITION
Norma Shirk – 1st ed.
TITLE: Things Go Wrong: Legal Minefields that Business Owners Hate But Have to Deal With
                        p. cm.
BUS060000 BUSINESS & ECONOMICS / Small Business
BUS025000 BUSINESS & ECONOMICS / Entrepreneurship
BUS024000 BUSINESS & ECONOMICS / Education

ISBN Paperback: 978-1-7324885-2-6
ISBN Hardcover: 978-1-7324885-3-3
ISBN eBook: 978-1-7324885-4-0

Distributed by CCRA Press
14   10 9 8 7 6 5 4 3 2 1

Printed in the United States of America

CCRA

CORPORATE
COMPLIANCE
RISK ADVISOR

In memory of Big Mike and Chris
Two great guys who left us too soon

Contents

INTRODUCTION

Every person who starts a business has a particular set of skills. That's what made you decide to take the plunge into entrepreneurship in the first place. But these skills rarely involve running the administrative or back-office part of a business. For example, you don't initially write down processes; you make everything up in the moment.

As a result, many new businesses falter as they begin to scale up when they add new services or products or new clients or customers which requires adding more staff. As you add more bells and whistles, including more people, complexity increases. If every process is in the owner's head rather than written down, there's no way to train new hires. If the owner makes off-the-cuff decisions about everything, a sense of unfairness creeps in and the whole operation begins to fall apart.

That's where this book comes in. This book sets out some basic compliance issues that business owners, HR managers and compliance officers should think about when starting a new business or scaling up to a larger size. This book can't answer all your questions, but it might help you avoid some common pitfalls that new business and small business owners face.

To illustrate some of the common pitfalls, I created Camilla Flowers, a/k/a Cam the Glam, and her business The Glamor Guide. Cam the Glam has many adventures in small business ownership that explain the boring legal and compliance concepts discussed in this book. Cam the Glam debuted in a series of social media posts while I was finishing this book because she was too much fun to keep to myself.

Cam's adventures prove the most important point for you to remember: Things go wrong. In fact, most back-office structures are created *after* things go wrong. This is particularly true in the HR world involving employment practices. So set aside any notions you have about perfection.

But don't let the risks stop you. As an engineer once told me, "If you thought about all the things that can go wrong, nothing would ever get built."

Remember that you don't have to be an expert on each area of the company's operations or on every law that affects the legal compliance of the company. But you do need to be familiar with the most common compliance issues that arise and where to go look for more information when you need it. Eventually, you will be able to outsource some of these compliance issues to professionals with specialized knowledge. But you still need to be able to understand the issues to discuss them intelligently and protect your business.

RISKS

Let's begin with a look at the big picture of corporate compliance. There is no such thing as a risk-free world. Every business activity carries some level of risk, just as our individual actions carry a personal risk to our lives or livelihood. Compliance is about recognizing those risks and managing them in order to keep the risks at an acceptable level so that the business can function effectively.

Business risks can be organized into four broad categories.

Hazard: Unforeseen, crises outside normal operations, such as tornadoes and floods. Of course, as climate change brings more severe weather extremes, natural disasters will become more common, making these risks more costly to mitigate.

Financial: Changing market conditions that affect a company's revenue, such as economic downturns or new government regulations that could change how you run your business and what you estimated in your budget.

Reputational: Damage to the company's image for things like fraudulent accounting practices by senior management, selling unsafe products or incurring a database breach that reveals confidential customer information. These days, you can include backing the "wrong" side of a social or political issue, as social media campaigns might target your company's sales.

Operational: Daily business activities, such as a lack of internal controls that cause losses to the company, out-of-control expenses or cyber-attacks that interrupt business activities.

To mitigate risk, a company creates policies and processes to avoid obvious mistakes and violations of the law. Of course, too many policies and procedures will stifle innovation and reduce the ability to make money. So, effective compliance policies balance caution and security against acceptable levels of risk that hopefully lead to income growth. After all, founding a company is one of the biggest risks any person can take since we know most fail within the initial five years of operations.

As an owner or as an employee working with senior management to create effective policies to mitigate these risks, remember that your compliance role is two-fold. First, you must be able to look at the risks currently faced by the company and create policies and procedures that mitigate those risks. Second, you must be able to look at future risks that your company and its industry will face so that you can begin adapting your company's policies and financial plans to meet the new compliance risks.

> When risks are ignored, failure often follows. Blockbuster stuck with its business model of costly rental and late-return fees even as consumers switched to the more consumer-friendly policies of Netflix. Blockbuster soon went bust. Meanwhile, Netflix has adapted repeatedly as consumers moved into streaming movies. Now Netflix's model is under threat from many other streaming services, including those offered by Apple and Disney.

This means you need to stay informed about current events, particularly legislative actions by Congress and the state legislatures in states where your company sells its products or services. You'll also need to stay informed about the actions of the regulatory agencies that affect your business at the federal and state levels. Stay up to date on the business climate for your state, the federal government and other regions of the world. As we'll discuss later, consumer privacy and internet sales mean that laws outside the U.S. may affect how you do business in the cloud. If you don't like to watch the news or lack the time, join a trade group for your industry that can provide updates.

A Brief Word on Priority of Law

You've probably noticed already that there are lots of laws coming at you from several levels of government. Which ones apply to your business? If these laws conflict, which should you follow? To answer these questions, it's necessary to digress briefly into a discussion of federalism, meaning how our government works.

Unless you're a lawyer or a political science professor, you probably haven't paid much attention to this sort of structural question since a high school civics class. But all that seeming drivel drummed into your head in class is suddenly important if you want your business to avoid negative scrutiny by the government, from the local folks to the feds. Every level of government has a say in how your business operates and how it is taxed thanks to our system of federalism.

A federalist system has layers of government with each layer having authority to create and enforce laws. The U.S. has a national government, fifty state governments, and county and city governments within each state. But as the layers descend from the federal level to the state level and then to local governments, the jurisdictional scope narrows. Federal laws apply to everyone within the boundaries of the U.S., but county or city ordinances only apply to people living, working or doing business in that county or city.

A model of how this looks follows on the next page.

Federal laws
Apply in all states

⬇

State laws
Apply only within a state

⬇

County or City ordinances
Apply only within county/city

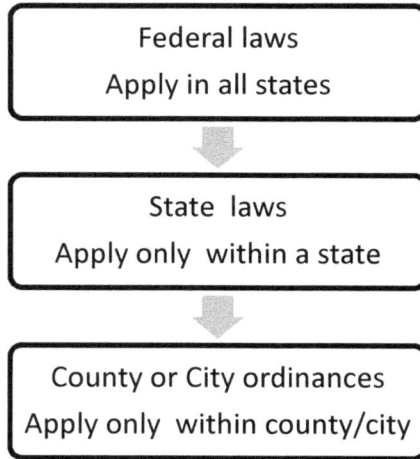

Federal Level

The national government is based in Washington, D.C. and consists of three co-equal branches of government: the executive (the President of the U.S. or POTUS), the legislature (U.S. Congress) and the judicial branch which is headed by the Supreme Court of the U.S. (SCOTUS).

Actions by any of these three branches of the federal government apply to every state and person in this country. In a process that many find more revolting than making sausage, members of Congress propose a law and if it passes both houses of Congress, the proposed law goes to the POTUS. If the POTUS signs the proposed law, a new federal law or statute is created, or in the lingo, is enacted.

But a new statute is just the first step. The laws are enforced through regulations written by federal regulatory agencies and departments. Federal regulators that your business will come to love and hate are the Department of Health and Human Services (HHS), Department of Labor (DOL) or one of its subsidiaries like the Wage & Hour Division (WHD) or the Occupational Health & Safety Administration (OSHA), the Internal Revenue Service (IRS), and the Federal Trade Commission (FTC). There are many other regulatory agencies and departments that focus on particular industries or issues, such as the Department of Transportation (DOT) or the Environmental Protection Agency (EPA).

The federal courts handle lawsuits which arise from the enforcement of federal laws which involve interstate commerce, or, in certain cases, are between citizens of different states. For example, ABC Corporation is incorporated in Tennessee and it sues a company based in Texas for millions of dollars in damages. There is a chance that the lawsuit could be fought out in federal court rather than a Tennessee or Texas state court.

> Pay a clever lawyer to draft your company contracts so that it is easier to sue or defend a lawsuit in the jurisdiction that you choose for your convenience. Your convenience usually means limiting your travel costs or finding a state with laws that are friendly to what your business does.

State Level

The U.S. consists of 50 states (and a few territories not discussed here) and each state must follow the laws established at the federal level. But each state also has an executive (the governor), a legislative (called the General Assembly in Tennessee) and a judicial branch of courts. The actions of these state governmental entities apply to the residents of and visitors to that particular state and to any business operating in that state.

Each state also has regulatory agencies that often mirror the federal agencies. For example, Tennessee's version of OSHA is called the Tennessee Occupational Health & Safety Administration (TOSHA).

A business operates in a state if it has a bricks and mortar location in the state or if it sells a service or product via the internet to people or businesses in that state. So if your company is planning to sell nationally, you'll need a compliance department that keeps up with changes to the laws of each state where you sell your company's products or services.

County and City Level

Each state is further divided into counties and cities which have authority to create laws, known as ordinances. These laws apply only to the residents of or visitors to that county or city and to the businesses operating there.

Now that we've breezed through federalism, check out the Appendix at the end of this book, which has a list of key regulatory agencies. County and city information is omitted here but can be found by Googling their names or via the links on a state government's website.

Summary

Your business will interact with each level of government described above. We'll be looking at some of these interactions later. For now, let's look at a brief description of your business's corporate structure.

CORPORATE STRUCTURE

We'll look at each key function of a company in more detail a little later in this book. For now, take a look at the chart below. The chart probably looks simplistic compared to the actual organizational chart of companies where you have worked. But no matter how the organizational chart is sliced, diced, and spread across the page, a corporation's activities will fall into one of the functions on this chart.

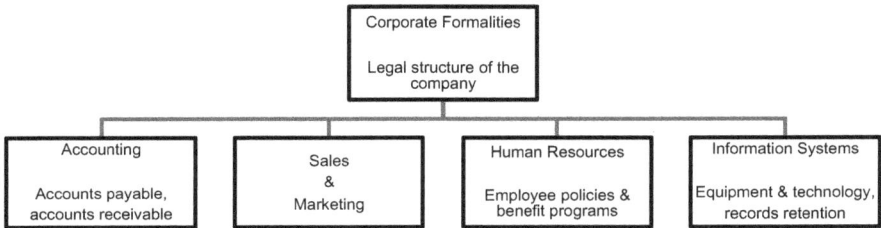

Corporate Formalities
Legal structure of the company

Accounting	Sales & Marketing	Human Resources	Information Systems
Accounts payable, accounts receivable		Employee policies & benefit programs	Equipment & technology, records retention

The majority of the remainder of this book looks at each of these functional areas of the company. Each of these areas has risks that must be mitigated by an effective corporate compliance program. For each of these areas, we will examine risks that are common to every business. We will also look at some commonly used internal controls to mitigate these risks.

We'll begin by looking at corporate formalities as it is the first step in setting up any business.

SETTING UP YOUR BUSINESS

Choosing a Name

What was the first step to setting up your business? Probably your first step was deciding on the name of the company. That's when you hit your first snag. Your wonderful new company name may already be taken by another business. So before you have business cards printed with the new company name, you need to check if your preferred company name is available.

In Tennessee, you can do a "Name Availability Search" on the website of the Tennessee Secretary of State's Office (www.tn.gov/sos). In the query box on the home page, enter the query "I want to check availability of name for business" and follow the on-line prompts to search their database to see if your chosen name is available.

If your chosen name is available, you may want to pay a fee to reserve the right to use the name. For example, you decide that you want to hang on to the name but you need a little more time to talk to a lawyer about the structure of your business. You decide to pay the fee to reserve your chosen company name. You are not required to take this step but filings with the TN SOS are first come, first served. So, this option prevents someone from filing ahead of you and grabbing the name you want to use while you're still getting organized. The name reservation is time-limited though, so be prepared to register your business soon after reserving the name.

> Avoid a common annoyance by creating several possible names for your business. Sometimes the name you want to use is already being used by another business. Or your preferred name may sound too similar to the name of another company. If you create several possible names for your business, you will surely think of one that is not already in use.

Legal Structure of the Company

Aside from the company name, the most critical step is to decide on a legal structure for your business. As a general rule, the legal structure is rarely changed after the business is set up. There are several options and each comes with its own risks and rewards.

Sole Proprietor or "Doing Business As" (d/b/a)

Many small, cash-strapped start-up companies begin as a d/b/a. A "d/b/a" may also be called the "assumed name." The name of the company would look like "Cam Flowers, d/b/a The Glam Guide." This is known as a sole proprietor, meaning there is one owner who makes every decision. The business owner could open a bank account in the name of "The Glam Guide" and begin operating as a business.

> Camilla "Cam" Flowers has a new business, taking wealthy people on urban safaris to high-end stores and on expensive adventures, like weekend trips at luxury spas where they can slurp Perrier water or 60-year-old scotch.
>
> She can't decide what legal structure is best for her business and right now, she's the only person working for the business. So, she's beginning as a d/b/a. Her business registers with the Tennessee Secretary of State (SOS) under the "assumed name" of The Glam Guide. It will be listed in their records as Camilla Flowers, d/b/a The Glam Guide.

The reward of this type of business structure is that there are few to no legal formalities.

You won't need to hold board of director meetings because your business won't have a board. You also won't need to hold shareholder meetings because you're the only shareholder. Of course, you could hold meetings with yourself but the people at the coffee shop might think you're weird.

The biggest risk of this structure is that there is no protection for the owner's personal assets. That's because from a legal viewpoint, Cam Flowers and The Glam Guide are the same "person." So if the business gets sued, it's the same as if Camilla gets sued and her personal assets are at risk. Her personal bank account, her car, and her house could be taken to cover payment of any claim against The Glam Guide.

This risk is the main reason most business owners choose to incorporate their businesses. Incorporating a business means that there is another legal "person", the business itself, which is liable for any judgments, rather than the owner's personal assets. Here's what Cam would face if she incorporates her business.

C Corporations (C-Corps)

This is the most common sort of corporate structure because there are no limits to the number of owners, meaning investors (called shareholders), in the business. If Cam Flowers chooses this legal structure, her business would be "The Glam Guide, Inc."

> Camilla Flowers decides to set up her company as a C-Corp. Her business is registered with the Tennessee SOS under the name The Glam Guide, Inc. She needs to file the company's Articles of Incorporation with the Tennessee SOS and pay the filing fee.

The reward of this type of legal structure is that the business owners can protect their personal assets from claims against the company. For example, the business entity is the legal "person" that takes out loans for business purposes and is on the hook to repay the money. Please note that with a new business, the bank or credit union will most likely require one or more individual business owners to sign a personal guaranty to repay the loan if the business doesn't. This protects the bank, which is relying on the individual owners' creditworthiness because the new business has no credit history.

Of course, these legal protections come with more rules, known as corporate formalities. For example, a C-corporation must have a board of directors that sets broad strategy for the business and oversees the actions of the company officers.

A corporation must also adopt bylaws which provide the legal rules for how the business will operate. By-laws are based on the statutory requirements which spell out the following:

1. Qualifications to be a corporate officer and the responsibilities of each officer. In other words, a job description for senior management-level positions.

2. Who may serve on the board of directors and how they are elected. Board seats are usually given to major shareholders, meaning investors in the business.
3. The number of times the board of directors must meet each year.
4. Who may invest in the business and how shares of stock will be given to the shareholders.
5. The date for the annual shareholders meeting and how they are notified of the meeting.
6. How the company will replace an officer or director if the individual retires, dies, resigns or is fired (in the case of an officer).
7. How the corporation will wind down its operations if it ceases to exist due to a merger with another company or bankruptcy. The business can also be administratively closed by the government for failing to comply with the law, including failing to hold required board or shareholder meetings or failing to pay taxes.

Corporations are also legally required to maintain a written record of what the corporation decided to do and why they did it. The written record is known as the corporate minutes and they are a summary of the issues discussed and the decisions made at each board meeting and each shareholder meeting.

At each board or shareholder meeting, the members are presented with "resolutions" which require a vote. Resolutions are the issues on which a formal vote is needed because the company is creating legal liability for the decisions made. For example, the board must vote to authorize the company president (or another officer) to sign a contract or to buy another business. So the resolution will be presented with "delegations of authority" for the officers.

> Roberts Rules of Order is a slim little book that explains how to present a resolution and a motion for the vote. These rules were first established in 1876 to ensure that all concerned parties, from board members to shareholders, are treated fairly.

Most resolutions include a summary of the reason a vote is needed then set out the specific question on which the directors or shareholders will vote. Before the vote, there must be a motion with a specific yes or no question that the board of directors or shareholders can approve, reject, or table for later discussion. The minutes should include the text of the actual resolution and whether the resolution is adopted or rejected or tabled for further discussion.

> Cam Flowers likes wearing feather boas when greeting new customers. Boas make her feel airy and light, like an actress from Hollywood's golden era of the 1930's.
>
> She presents a resolution to her board of directors that will authorize her to buy as many new feather boas as she needs for business purposes.
>
> She's not as risqué as Josephine Baker in her feathers, but Cam's adult children are board members and they've been embarrassed for years by Mom's boas, which they think make her look like an over-the-hill stripper. They vote "no" on the resolution. The minutes show that the resolution was voted down.

As you can see, there are many more requirements that must be followed for this type of legal structure and that means many more grounds on which the company can be sued. For example, an incorporated business that fails to hold regular shareholder meetings or to maintain the corporate minutes can be sued for failing to follow its own rules or the laws that apply to every corporation.

Another downside is that both the business and the individual owners and investors will pay taxes on their income from the business. However, the business can reduce its tax bill through allowed deductions of expenses and investments in things like new equipment.

If the company makes a profit, it can issue a dividend on the shares of its stock. The dividend is paid to the shareholders who must report it on their individual income tax statement. But dividends are taxed at a lower rate than income from wages. This encourages shareholders to continue investing.

Many business owners recognize that being able to protect their personal property from liability for claims against the business far outweighs the downside of taxes. With a clever, but honest, accountant, your business can sail through the tax liability issues.

> Even if you choose to not use the C-Corp structure, consider adopting some of its requirements, like officer qualifications, how to replace officers (and yourself as CEO or president), and how the company will cease operations. Answering these questions in advance will reduce your heartburn later when a crisis hits.

S Corporation (S-Corp)

Another option for an owner is to incorporate as an S-corporation. An S-Corp operates much like a C-Corp in that there must be a board of directors, regular board meetings, an annual shareholder meeting and corporate minutes.

But there are notable differences. First of all, an S-Corp is limited to a maximum of 100 shareholders. Due to the shareholder limit, S-Corps are a favorite of family-run businesses because they are not looking for outside investors to fund their activities.

> Cam Flowers wants to create a business that she will eventually pass along to her children or to her cat if her family continues to disappoint her. She sets up an S-Corp, The Glam Guide, Inc., in which each child owns a piece of the business. If the business does well, they each get a little extra income. If the business does poorly, they each get a possible tax deduction for their business loss.
>
> Her business registers with the Tennessee SOS under the name The Glam Safari Guide, Inc.

An S-Corp works like a cross between a corporation and a partnership. This difference is easiest to illustrate with how the taxes are paid. The S-Corp's profit (or loss) flows through to the personal income tax statement of the individual shareholders just like in a partnership. However, the S-Corp is also taxed as a business. In Tennessee, that means the S-Corp must pay the state's franchise and excise tax and the shareholders are taxed on company profit even if no dividend is paid to them. Some people view this arrangement as double-taxation. As a result, non-family businesses tend to choose the LLC corporate structure.

Limited Liability Company (LLC)

An LLC is probably the most popular corporate structure for smaller businesses. An LLC allows the owners, called members, to protect their personal assets from liability for the business. But an LLC has more flexibility than a C-Corp or an S-Corp because there are fewer statutory requirements for setting it up and maintaining it.

LLC's come in a couple of flavors. There are single member LLC's with only one owner and there are multi-member LLC's.

> Cam Flowers decides to create an LLC in which her children are co-owners. Since there is more than one owner, it is a multi-member LLC. Her business is registered with the Tennessee SOS under the name The Glam Guide, LLC as a multi-member LLC.

An LLC does not have by-laws. Instead, it has an operating agreement which covers the same issues that by-laws cover. The operating agreement is the only legal document to explain how the owners will resolve their disputes or terminate the business.

It is possible to start an LLC without an operating agreement. But if there is more than one owner, it would be a stupid and unnecessary risk to try to save money by not hiring a lawyer to draft this agreement. Think of the operating agreement as a business pre-nuptial agreement.

It is much cheaper to pay a lawyer to draft an operating agreement when everyone is still optimistic about the future than to pay a lawyer to defend a lawsuit after everyone has amnesia about what they thought and said at the time the business was formed. Trust me on this one!

> Cam Flowers sets up The Glam Guide, LLC with her children. Since the ownership is all in the family, Cam doesn't pay a lawyer to create an operating agreement.
>
> Years later her children decide that mom needs to retire and they try to push her out of the company she created.
>
> Without an operating agreement, there is no orderly way for her kids to remove her and their incessant sibling rivalries end up destroying the company.
>
> (Read *Bleak House*, by Charles Dickens for a literary version of family wealth destruction caused by incessant bickering over who gets to inherit.)

A downside to an LLC is that it can be a bit confusing on taxes. If only cne person owns the LLC, then the business is akin to a sole proprietorship and the profit or losses flow through to the owner's personal income tax return. If the LLC has several owners, then the business profit or losses can be handled as if the business is a partnership, meaning profit or loss pass through to their personal income statements. Alternatively, the LLC's profit or loss can be taken by the corporation. That is confusing and can rise up to bite the unwary during the initial tax season.

But regardless of the tax consequences, there are still benefits to setting up an LLC. It can protect the owner's personal assets from liability for claims against the company. If the tax consequences worry you, talk to your CPA or the attorney who is drafting your documents to help you understand the risks and rewards of an LLC.

Partnership

A partnership is a very old business structure that is less popular these days except in certain industries, such as real estate investment companies and professional firms like law firms and CPA firms. Partners can be real people (living, breathing humans) or another corporate entity. The upside is that partnerships have a lot of leeway in deciding how they will operate. Much like the LLC operating agreement, the partnership will have a partnership agreement.

Partnerships also come in several flavors. There are limited liability partnerships and limited partnerships. If you think you would like to use this business format, pay the required legal fees for a long chat with a lawyer who can explain how the different partnership structures work and whether this is a good legal structure based on your specific business goals.

> Cam Flowers decided long ago that her children are ungrateful whiners who don't deserve a piece of her action. She ignores the kids and sets up a partnership with her two best friends. The business is registered with the Tennessee SOS under the name The Glam Guide, LLP.

Partnerships don't have by-laws; they have partnership agreements. A partnership agreement describes how the business will operate, which partner is responsible for what and how each partner's interest can be bought out if the partner dies, wants to quit or the other partners vote her/him off the island. As with the LLC's operating agreement, it's the only way to legally establish an orderly way to run the business and wind it down.

The major drawback to a partnership is that there is usually "joint and several" liability. Each owner of the business is liable for all claims against the business. If a partner is unable or unwilling to pay a portion of the partnership's liabilities, the other partners will have to cover the entire amount.

> Cam Flowers set up a partnership with her two best friends called The Glam Guide, LLP. Six months later, one partner decides that she prefers being glamorous as a hobby, not a business. Her interests in the partnership are bought out by the remaining partners.
>
> The following tax season, Cam discovers that her other business partner emptied the bank account and disappeared to a tropical island. Cam is on the hook to pay the taxes and any other claims against the business because she's the only partner still around to face the music.

Common Risks

For corporations, the most common risk, particularly for a small business, is a failure to follow its own rules. For example, small businesses often fail to follow their rules on holding shareholder and board meetings. As a result, corporate officers like the president take actions that are not approved by the board or the shareholders. That can have dreadful consequences for the business.

The most common risk for an LLC or a partnership is that the owners ignore the importance of creating an operating agreement or partnership agreement. So there's no road map to explain who is responsible for what and how they'll agree on spending the money for the business. If the owners have a misunderstanding, the situation can quickly escalate into broken friendships and a failing business.

Another risk is not holding board or shareholder meetings as required by law. At smaller companies, senior management tends to stay busy with daily operations and might forget to consistently hold required meetings or get approval for actions that they take. The risk is that a court will decide that the legal structure is a sham because corporate formalities were not followed regularly, and that means that the owners could be held personally liable for corporate debts and obligations.

Piercing the Corporate Veil

Smaller companies with only one or two owners face a constant legal threat known as "piercing the corporate veil." Piercing the corporate veil happens when the company's creditors successfully argue that the corporate structure is a sort of sham or false front for the owners.

When the corporate veil is pierced, owners become individually liable for the company's debts and their personal assets may be used to pay off the company's creditors. To limit this risk, know what the law requires for your company's structure, such as holding regular board meetings and shareholder meetings and keeping minutes of the decisions taken at each of these meetings. Then follow the requirements.

Cam Flowers and her adult children own the business she created. They rarely hold formal board or shareholder meetings, preferring to discuss business decisions over fried chicken on Sunday afternoons. Everyone is too stuffed from eating roast beast and pecan pie to think about writing down a summary of what they discussed and what they decided to do. During football season, they usually fall asleep in front of the TV. So there are no corporate minutes.

Then the company is sued by an angry customer who complains that her upscale shopping trip wasn't glamorous because she didn't spend much money. During the discovery phase of the lawsuit, the customer's lawyer discovers that Cam and her kids never followed the legal requirements for being a corporation.

The lawyer argues that the corporation is a sham and that the customer should be allowed to pierce the corporate veil. If the judge agrees, Cam and her kids will be personally liable for any judgment won by the angry customer.

Warning! Don't risk your personal reputation and your financial future by ignoring the rules that apply to your business's legal structure. Hire a detail-obsessed compliance person and make that person responsible for ensuring the company follows the rules. Paying an employee who nags you about following the rules is always less expensive than the cost of defending a lawsuit.

Summary of Corporate Legal Structure

Before deciding on the "best" corporate structure for your new business, please spend some time creating a list of your goals for the business.

Then talk to a lawyer who regularly helps businesses incorporate. The lawyer can explain the pros and cons of each legal structure and how best to protect your personal assets from liability for what the business does. You should also talk to a certified public accountant (CPA) to learn about how each type of business is taxed.

By now, you've noticed that just setting up your company involves weighing risks such as personal liability and taxes. Every business action, or inaction, carries risks. But let's admit the truth: if you wanted to avoid risks, you could have stayed in your old job and worried about being laid off or having a rotten boss who made your life miserable. It's all about choosing what you want to worry about late at night when you can't sleep.

> Starting a business is risky. But admit it: If you wanted to avoid risks, you could have stayed in your old job and worried about being laid off or having a rotten boss who made your life miserable. It's all about choosing what you want to worry about late at night when you can't sleep.

Notifying the Government That You're in Business

You've now jumped over the initial hurdles of setting up your business. You've picked a name for the business and decided on the legal structure of the business. Now, it is time to let the government know that you're in business. First, you'll need to register as a new business with the Tennessee Secretary of State which is done on-line at www.tn.gov/sos.

Once you have a company name registered with the SOS, the next critical task is to create your business' tax accounts. Your business will have tax accounts at both the federal and state levels.

Apply for a federal tax ID at www.irs.gov. The IRS wants to hear from you and makes it relatively painless to register via their website. (This is probably the only time that you will be happy and optimistic when interacting with the IRS.) A federal tax ID is known as an

Employer Identification Number (EIN) or a Federal Employer Identification Number (FEIN).

At the state level in Tennessee, your business will also need to set up a tax account, known as a "TNTAP" account, with the Tennessee Department of Revenue (www.tn.gov/revenue). Click on the homepage tab "Taxes" and you'll see a list of state taxes on businesses. Your business will be responsible for paying franchise and excise (F&E) taxes or sales and use (S&U) taxes.

> Make sure that your application for an EIN spells your company's name *exactly* as it appears in your Tennessee Secretary of State filing for your company's name. If the names don't match exactly, you will live a miserable business life trying to convince the federal government and the state government to recognize a different spelling of your company's name. Every business lawyer and CPA has a horror story about this one.

> Cam Flowers registered her business with the Tennessee Secretary of State's office under the name "The Glam Guide, Inc." Unfortunately, she was in a hurry when she applied for an EIN with the IRS and listed the name as "The Glam Guide, Incorporated".
>
> Months later, Cam contacts the IRS for assistance. The IRS representative is unable to pull up any information about her company under the name "The Glam Guide, Inc."

Additionally, if you are hiring employees immediately, you will need to create an employer account with the Tennessee Department of Labor & Workforce Development so that you can notify the state when you hire an employee. Depending on the type of business, you may also need a license from the city or county government in which your business is based. We'll look at Tennessee state taxes later.

Summary of Notifying the Government

The federal, state and local governments will be happy to congratulate you on your new business. So be sure to invite them to the party by registering your business with them. At tax time, they will still be happy for you even if you are not happy with them. As we'll see in the next section about accounting, each level of government will want to collect taxes owed by your business.

ACCOUNTING

Simplistically, accounting is about money in (accounts receivable) and money out (accounts payable) of the company. The money coming in must exceed the money going out or you'll quickly face a transition to a new career. Many companies fail in their first year when the business runs out of money. Most fail before their fifth birthday.

Running out of money happens for a couple of reasons. Most commonly, new businesses are undercapitalized, meaning they don't have enough money to support business operations until sales pick up and the lack of funds causes them to fold. Sadly, this is most true of women-owned businesses, who tend to start out underfunded. The second most common reason is runaway expenses, meaning more money is going out the door than is coming in the door.

> Don't buy the bling or live a Rich & Famous Lifestyle until your business has a sustainable revenue stream and makes a profit. Save a percentage of the income in a corporate rainy-day fund so that you can cover a minimum of 6 months of expenses even if no customer payments are received.

Unless you have a degree in accounting or are a CPA, don't try to understand the intricacies of accounting rules. Hire an accountant or a CPA firm to handle the details. As a business owner or as a corporate compliance person, you just need to be able to recognize the points of risk.

Tracking Your Money

The first rule of accounting in business is to track the money as it flows in and then out of your company. If you start your business with a budget that is thinner than a shoestring, an Excel spreadsheet can help you track the money coming in and going out. But you'll want to upgrade to accounting software as soon as possible. Quickbooks and Freshbooks are two cloud-based small business accounting software programs that allow you to track your income, track your expenses, and prepare client invoices. There are many other options, too, including programs that are industry-specific.

These programs have built-in standard templates for budgeting and profit and loss statements. These reports will help you track the financial health of your company and will also simplify your life at tax time because they can generate all the information your certified public accountant (CPA) needs to prepare your tax forms.

QuickBooks, FreshBooks, and similar accounting programs are theoretically designed for use by non-accountant people. The vendors provide on-line support and tutorials to help you get set up and running well. However, your CPA firm likely has an "expert" on staff who is trained by the vendor and who can assist you. If you'd rather fight the monsters under the bed than figure out your accounting software, hire a bookkeeper or an assistant who is good at this, or outsource accounting. CPA firms often offer bookkeeping services to their small business clients. Hire them and pay them first each month. It's worth the peace of mind.

Cam read the marketing blurb on the website and decided the DIY version of QuickBooks was for her. She was trying to keep overhead costs down so there would be more profit. Besides, how hard could it be?

Cam immediately logged into her new on-line account, eager to begin the set up. And that's when she hit the first snag. She needed to pick a type of business but there was no category for Glam guides. Cam opened a bottle of wine and genteelly sipped as she scrolled through the business options.

She accidentally hit "Enter" and her business selection was complete. Now she had to set up expense categories. She poured a second glass of wine. Before long only the "Ask Accountant" category looked like a good option.

An hour later, Cam opened another bottle of wine as she cursed QuickBooks, accounting, and DIY options. Tomorrow, when she sobers up, Cam plans to call her accountant to ask how much it would cost for their bookkeeping services.

Common Risks

The most common risk in the Accounting Department of any company is that money will leave the company in ways that it shouldn't. Examples include embezzlement, such as inflating expense accounts or creating fictitious payroll entries, or theft of company property. To mitigate these risks, an effective compliance program will include internal controls. Some common internal controls are:

- Ensure that one person prepares checks to pay vendor invoices or the payroll, but a different person signs the checks. Alternatively, if your company pays by electronic transfer, have one person prepare a list of the names and amounts and have a second person authorize the payments.

- Reconcile the monthly bank statement yourself, if you're the owner, until your company has the income to hire a chief financial officer (CFO) to handle these tasks. But as the owner, you still need to spot check the business bank accounts and financial statements. After all, it's your money, livelihood and reputation that is at stake so follow the money.

- Reimburse expenses only when there is a receipt that can be matched to a legitimate business expense. You might want to set a minimum amount. For example, any expense over $10 or $50 must be accompanied by a receipt.

- Require prior authorization for payments over a designated dollar amount (e.g., $1000, $5000).

- Outsource your payroll and tax payments to a CPA firm. They are professionally trained to handle these financial matters. They also have malpractice insurance to reimburse your business if one of their people goes rogue and gets sticky fingers.

- Ensure that the company owners, including yourself if you're an owner, don't use the corporate bank account as a piggy bank to cover personal expenses.

- Routinely audit the company's accounts payable and accounts receivable records to spot any odd activity. If your business has a bricks and mortar location, you should regularly audit the inventory, from office furniture to postage stamps. Many CPA firms offer auditing services.

Some of these internal controls may seem unnecessary, particularly when you're busy with other aspects of your business. But your financial life is on the line so don't delegate financial responsibility and then ignore your bank accounts. Review all financial reports for your business on a regular basis.

In a previous career, I investigated employee dishonesty claims. I saw many businesses that were looted into insolvency by a trusted employee who was given authority to write checks and reconcile the bank statements each month. In each case, the company owner had failed to implement the most basic controls to avoid the risk of loss.

As a business owner, your money and reputation is on the line. Trust your people to do their jobs. But you need to set aside time every week to review your company's finances to verify that all is well. In addition, you should review your company's finances every quarter with your CPA.

Another common risk for companies is fiddling with the company's financial reports, whether to artificially inflate the company's stock value (for publicly-traded companies) or to manipulate the amount of taxes owed by the corporation. Accounting rules are diabolically convoluted and honest disputes can arise between the company and its shareholders or with the IRS or state revenue department. Honest disputes about your business's taxable income and expense deductions are acceptable. Fraud is not.

To mitigate financial skullduggery, publicly traded companies must comply with the Sarbanes-Oxley Act (SOX). SOX was enacted in 2002 after several high profile accounting scandals at publicly-traded companies. (Do an internet search of "Enron" or "MCI" to see why Congress rushed to enact SOX.) Some key rules in SOX require publicly traded companies to implement internal controls such as:

- Creating an audit subcommittee to the Board of Directors which is responsible for overseeing the internal accounting staff and reviewing the outside auditor reports. The subcommittee members must have accounting or financial industry backgrounds that ensure they understand the financial reports they are reviewing.

(Helpful hint: If the reports are so complicated no one understands them, dig deeper. Overly-complicated reports may be a sign of fraud).

- Retaining a CPA firm as an outside auditor to review and certify the company's tax returns and securities filings with the Securities and Exchange Commission (SEC).
- Prohibiting that same CPA firm from preparing tax statements for the business while simultaneously performing audit services. (This is the issue that destroyed the reputation and much of the business model of the CPA firm Arthur Anderson, which offered dual services to Enron).
- Implementing an internal whistleblower system for employees to report alleged financial abuses to the Board of Directors without fear of retaliation.
- Requiring the chief executive officer or president and the chief financial officer to certify the accuracy of all company financial reports. The CEO and CFO have personal liability, including a maximum $2 million fine and a maximum 25 years in prison, if they knowingly certify false financial information. (This is the part that caused so much uproar when the law was enacted).

SOX does not apply to privately-held companies, which means your small business won't have to meet these requirements. However, privately-held companies can use SOX as a guide for best practices. Whether you work for a publicly-traded company or for a privately-held company, as an owner or a compliance officer, you should become familiar with the basics of SOX.

For a best practices checklist that covers SOX and other tax laws, look at IRS Publication 4557 *"Safeguarding Taxpayer Data: A Guide for Your Business."* By IRS standards, it's actually user-friendly. Your CPA can explain which of the laws discussed in the booklet will apply to your business and what you need to do to comply with those laws.

Taxes – They Want Your Money

Taxation occurs at three levels: federal, state and county or city. That's because each of these levels of government have a legal responsibility to provide services that benefit the public. That means the government needs to levy taxes to pay for street lights and roads, installing utilities and staffing courts that protect your legal interests in your business.

Federal taxes

Every business and business owner must pay federal income taxes. Taxes may be offset with business deductions. Federal tax laws and regulations change constantly so your best investment as a business owner is to pay a CPA firm to prepare your tax returns.

If your business has W-2 employees, the company will need to pay quarterly payroll taxes by filing IRS Form 941 and submitting the appropriate amount of taxes. Payroll taxes cover FICA, FUTA, and SUTA. If you are the only worker for your business, you will owe a quarterly self-employment tax covering the same payroll taxes.

Even if you have only one W-2 employee or are the sole employee, do yourself a giant favor and hire a CPA firm to handle payroll and self-employment taxes. The reward of saving a few bucks now is never worth the risk of drawing the negative attention of the IRS.

What's Included in the Payroll Tax?

FICA	Federal Insurance Contribution Act	The total tax is 15.3% of W-2 wages. All wages up to $160,200 are subject to this tax which is split between the employee and employer with each contributing: 6.2% Social Security tax (for SSA retirement). 1.45% Medicare tax (Part A coverage of Medicare). Wages exceeding $200,000 are subject to an additional 0.9% Medicare tax paid by the employee only. Independent contractors (1099's) or self-employed individuals pay the entire 15.3%.
FUTA	Federal Unemploy- ment Tax Act	The 6.0% payroll tax is paid solely by the employer on the initial $7,000 earned by an employee. Independent contractors or self-employed individuals don't pay FUTA and are not eligible for unemployment insurance payments if they become unemployed. (Eligibility was temporarily available during the covid pandemic.)

SUTA	State Unem-ployment Tax Authorities	Payroll tax paid by the employer based on a rate set by the state in which the employee works. Tennessee's maximum tax is 10% on the initial $7,000 earned by the employee. This tax goes into the state's unemployment fund. This is a state tax, but is included here because, like FICA and FUTA, it is based on the company's payroll. Independent contractors or self-employed individuals don't pay SUTA and are not eligible for unemployment insurance payments if they become unemployed.

State Taxes

In addition to the federal taxes payable to the IRS, your business will owe state taxes. State taxes in Tennessee fall into two broad categories: business taxes and employment-related taxes.

Business taxes include the franchise and excise (F&E) tax and the sales and use tax. A franchise tax is assessed on the value of real or tangible personal property. An excise tax is assessed on the net income of the company each tax year. Every corporation, LLC, and partnership operating in Tennessee will pay the Tennessee F&E tax, even if it's just the minimum taxable amount of $100.

In Tennessee, a sales tax is assessed against all retail sales, leases, or rentals in the state. Sales tax is now collected on internet sales. The sales tax is based on the amount of the sale or lease or rental and must be collected by the seller. The use tax must also be paid on the purchase of tangible personal property, such as computer software.

In Tennessee, a sales tax may also be assessed by the county and by the largest cities, Chattanooga, Knoxville, Memphis, and Nashville (Metro Davidson County). If your business is based in Davidson County (i.e., Metro Nashville), you will be paying the state sales tax *plus* the Davidson County/Metro Nashville sales tax. Since Nashville and Davidson County are one governmental entity, your business only pays one local sales tax.

> Tennessee has over 400 taxing jurisdictions ranging from the state to each county and city. Unless you have masochistic tendencies, there is no need to drive yourself insane trying to figure out which taxes are owed by your business. Hire a CPA firm and let them handle this stuff. Whatever your CPA charges you now will still cost you less than trying to fix it later.

Any businesses based in Tennessee selling products or services over the internet must collect sales tax on their internet sales. The rules changed in 2018 after the Tennessee Supreme Court ruled that the state could collect sales taxes on internet-based sales. Depending on the volume of sales, your company may be required to file and pay the sales tax monthly to the state.

As previously mentioned, businesses in Tennessee are also assessed employee-related taxes. One tax goes into the Unemployment Trust Fund which covers the payments made each month to qualified unemployed workers who are actively seeking another job.

Since January 1, 2019, employers in Tennessee are required to file a quarterly Premium and Wage Report with the Tennessee Department of Labor and Workforce Development. The report must be filed electronically through the employer's account with the Department at https://tnpaws.tn.gov. Companies that don't already have an employer account must complete Form LB-0441, "Report to Determine Status, Application for Employer Number." Go to www.tn.gov/workforce and follow the on-line prompts.

Another employee-related cost that seems like a tax is workers comp insurance which covers work-related injuries. Tennessee employers with five or more employees must pay into the workers compensation insurance fund. We'll talk more about workers comp later.

Do all these tax requirements sound confusing and depressing? Of course, they do! That's why it's important to hire a CPA firm to figure out how much money your business owes to the federal, state, and local tax authorities. A CPA is professionally trained to sort out these types of headaches. Meanwhile, you can get back to doing your day job running your company.

Licensing

It may seem odd to talk about licensing in the middle of a discussion about taxes. Here's a tip: government regulators can cruise the internet looking for violations. States and local governments are interested because if you lack a required business license, you might not be paying the correct amount of taxes. Of course, government workers usually wait for a complaint to be filed against your business.

The lack of a business license is often discovered when a grumpy client or customer files a complaint with the Better Business Bureau or the state agency that investigates consumer protection complaints. Paranoid competitors may also complain to a government regulator that issues licenses to businesses in your industry. One of the easiest allegations to investigate and confirm is whether your business is properly licensed.

Business licenses are most common in the retail industry for businesses that sell directly to individual consumers. Most licenses are issued by the state in which you sell your product or service. However, local governments like cities also issue business licenses. Some Tennessee examples of licensed businesses include residential roofing companies, plumbers, hair salons, mental health counselors, massage therapists, and the list goes on and on. One prominent financial magazine dubbed state licensing requirements the "License Raj."

The penalties for not having a required business license can be dire.

The state might assess cash penalties or shut down your business until you obtain a license. So give yourself some peace of mind. Before opening your doors, ask other business owners in the same industry or consult an attorney or CPA who regularly works on business issues for small business clients.

Summary of Accounting

The accounting department handles money in (accounts receivable) and money out (accounts payable) for your business. The department should also ensure that taxes are paid on time and in the correct amount. Don't sort through it alone. Find a clever, but honest, accountant. While the accountant figures out what your business owes the government, you'll be busy worrying about where your business will get the money to pay all these taxes.

SALES AND MARKETING

Sales and marketing are about generating revenue – income – for the company so that your business becomes sustainable. We all create businesses expecting to make buckets of money. We often imagine that customers or clients will flock to us to buy our product or service. If only it were that easy!

In order to sell your product or service, you need a target. Before you opened your business you should have answered the following questions. Who is your ideal client? How will you let them know that you're in business? How will you sell to them?

Your sales strategy starts before you create your business with figuring out.....
- Who is my ideal client?
- How will I let them know that I'm in business?
- What will I sell to them?
- How will I sell to them?

Books about how to sell anything to anyone are a sizable chunk of the book publishing industry. You can also hire sales coaches and strategists to help you develop your sales and marketing strategy. All these services are worthwhile. But only if you've answered the above questions.

You may also find that your initial business budget doesn't include a line item for hiring a sales coach. Don't despair. Creating the initial sales and marketing processes can be done without expert help. After your business has some money in the bank, find an expert to help you enhance your sales and marketing strategy so that your business can continue to grow.

> Design your marketing materials and sales pitch from your client's or customer's viewpoint. What's in it for them? Will your service or product save them time, or money, or make them the best-looking person on the planet? How can you help your clients or customers to achieve their goals? These questions will guide you in designing your marketing materials.

Sales Process v. Marketing Process

Sales and marketing are often used interchangeably but they are not the same.

Sales Process

A sales process is an internal document that explains your company's back-office processes for selling. It is a confidential, often proprietary, set of internal rules to be used only by you and your staff, whether W-2 employees or 1099 independent contractors. It explains how you will identify your potential client or customer based on your model of an ideal client.

It also explains how you will "vet" your client. Vetting the client means determining:

- How serious is this prospect about hiring your company?
- Does this prospect have the budget (i.e., money) to pay your fees or to buy your product?
- If your company is selling a service, will the prospective buyer accept your advice or fight you every step of the way?

The sales process also explains how you will on-board the client or customer. Will you require clients or customers to sign a sales contract outlining your scope of services? What information do you need from your client or customer to begin performing your services? If your company sells a product, how will you collect payment? What type of sales receipt will you give to customers? What customer information will you gather and how will you keep it secure?

Your sales process should cover the following:

1. How you will identify your client based on your ideal client profile.
2. Steps needed to vet the client, meaning ensuring they can pay you.
3. Steps for sending a proposal, obtaining a signed proposal and on-boarding the new client.
4. How your company will up-sell additional products or services, when appropriate.
5. Steps to be taken to terminate the client relationship when the work is completed or if the client fails to timely pay you.

Internet sales are booming for businesses of all sizes but trust may be low on both sides. A customer may be reluctant to pay before receiving the product or service. A company might be reluctant to ship a product or allow access to a service until payment is received. What does this mean for your small business?

It means you will need a reliable, secure payment method for your company's internet sales. Your business will be accepting credit card payments, which means you need a bank account linked to a vendor that can process credit card payments for your business. PayPal and Venmo are probably the best known of these services, but there are scores of others.

Finally, a sales process explains how you will wrap up your relationship with the client or customer. For example, you may want to sell additional services or products. You might need to fire your client or customer for non-payment or rejected payments, such as not-sufficient-funds bank checks or stolen credit cards or bankruptcy of the client or customer. The downside for small businesses can feel like a financial death sentence. So it's crucial to plan for the downside before it happens.

Marketing Process

A marketing process is an internal company document that looks outward to explain how you will let people know about your service or product. How does your ideal client/customer typically look for the product or service that you sell? What sort of marketing materials, such as brochures and business cards, will you need?

How will you convince buyers that your service or product helps solve their pain points? Do you plan to blog about your company's services or products? What social media accounts will you use to reach clients and customers? How often will you post fresh information? A marketing process is how you keep your company's service or product top of mind with potential clients or customers.

Your marketing strategy will depend on:

1. How does your company's service or product help them with a pain point?
2. Where does your ideal client or customer typically look for the product or service you are selling?
3. What marketing materials (brochures, business cards) will you need?
4. Which social media platforms are used by your clients or customers?

This is a lively area for compliance especially as we all grapple with the technological changes of digital marketing. We've come a long way since the old days of traveling shows peddling snake oil cures. Internet sales exceeded bricks-and-mortar store sales a few years ago and the covid-19 pandemic accelerated the transition.

Major tech companies, such as Amazon, Facebook, and Google use algorithms to track the details of every individual who visits their websites. Their algorithms can also track your visits to other websites through the use of "cookies". All this personal data about you as a consumer is then packaged for use by businesses, perhaps even your new business. It's the reason your company's website and blogs use particular words (Search Engine Optimization or SEO) to enhance the chances of moving up the list of search results so that you can sell more stuff.

That's all good for your on-line sales and it means that you may not need to hire a gaggle of traditional salespeople to pound the pavement for you. But you still need to be aware of a plethora of laws and regulations that protect "consumers" from flimflam artists and fraudsters, the modern version of snake oil salesmen. We'll look at some of the key ones below. As usual, don't forget that there are also industry-specific marketing laws for highly regulated industries, such as banking, insurance and professions like lawyers.

If you are responsible for compliance in one of the highly regulated industries, you can stay informed through industry publications, and industry-sponsored training, and so forth. For this book, we'll take a more generic approach, providing an overview.

> If these marketing questions seem depressingly complex, it's only because they are. Don't go it alone. Hire a social media or marketing consultant to help your company develop and implement a marketing process.

Branding

Every business has a brand, whether intentional or unintentional. It's best to make it intentional, of course. Examples of your company's brand are the name, the company logo, the colors and typeface you use in your marketing materials, your mission statement, and your company's reputation.

To protect your brand, you might want to copyright or trademark your logo so others can't use it or create something so similar that the two brands could be mistaken for each other. Obtaining a copyright or trademark requires filing legal documents which means you will need to hire an attorney who does intellectual property (IP) law. IP attorneys do not come cheap so you may need to wait to explore this option.

> Unless you're a magnificently creative person or in the marketing business, it's best to outsource the task of branding your company. When researching vendors, ask your friends who they use. Meet with several vendors to assess how easy they are to work with and whether their creative vision makes sense to you. Ask 2 – 3 vendors for proposals. It's not about the lowest price. It's about who offers the best "fit" for your company.

Another aspect of branding is your company's vision statement and mission statement. A vision statement sets out the future objectives of the company. A mission statement describes the current purpose and objectives of the company. Why create either of these statements?

> Cam's vision statement:
> I want to do good in the world.
>
> Cam's mission statement:
> Be the best urban safari glamor guide in the world.

A vision statement and a mission statement help you as the business owner to explain why you set up your company and who you want to serve. These statements are a guide for prospective clients or customers to decide whether to buy your company's service or product. These statements also help your team to understand your guiding principles for doing business.

Marketing in Person - Networking

The oldest marketing tool is networking, meaning showing up at business or social events and talking to people about what they do and what your company does. This allows you to spread the word about who is your company's ideal client. Networking efforts can begin before you officially open your doors to customers or clients. Networking builds buzz.

But before dashing out to every rubber chicken luncheon or summer barbeque hosted by a business or industry group, think about what you want to accomplish.

Most of us have an elevator pitch, a 30 – 60 second description of who we are and what we do. Most people rattle off their spiel at Mach speed. Distinguish yourself from the crowd at the next networking event.

Make your pitch sound natural by talking slower and by avoiding corporate-speak like "solutions" and "implementation." Everyone has a "solution." The millionth time you hear the word "solutions", your brain will feel as if it's dissolving.

Use plain English to explain why your company's product or service is the right choice for your audience or the people in their networks.

Think about where your ideal customer lives, works and plays. This will vary depending on the age range of your ideal client and the industry in which you operate. A tattoo parlor has a very different client in mind than a company selling home decor. Think about where your competitors lurk and how likely you are to be different from their target market.

Know why you're attending an event. For example, set a goal of meeting three new people. Have a couple of prepared questions, such as commenting on the room, the food, the weather or whatever. Ask the other person what they do and what they like best or least about it. Alternatively, you can set a goal of meeting at least one person who could be a potential referral source to your business or a potential customer.

> Whatever your ice breaker patter, don't be pushy or hog the conversation. If you catch yourself chattering about the details of every major business decision you've made during your brilliant career, you're not learning anything about the other person, except their tolerance threshold.

If you are shy and quiet, never fear. Set a goal of meeting three people and then leaving. Beg or bribe a member of your team or a friend who is an extrovert to go with you to do most the talking. Of course, it's a crutch! But it will help you get over your initial stage fright until you feel more confident about working a room. You might always feel uncomfortable when confronted with a room of people slurping watery cocktails; but it can become manageable with time.

> Cam knows her ideal client is an adult with lots of disposable income who wants an extraordinary experience instead of an ordinary shopping trip. To broaden the scope of her services, Cam is adding new glam adventures that she hopes will appeal to young adults who have generous allowances from their parents.
>
> To attract these upscale millennials and younger adults who want an "experience", she joins a local bungee jumping group and a hiking group. She also hangs out at hip bars and nightclubs, striking up conversations with people the same age as her adult children.

Marketing via the Internet

The internet is the great economic democratizer making it possible for new businesses to flourish at a very low entry cost. If your business is not on the web, it will lack legitimacy in the eyes of potential clients or customers. At a minimum your new business will need a website. Websites are hosted on platforms; the most well-known are GoDaddy and WordPress. If you outsource marketing, the marketing team can advise you on which platform offers the most features needed by your business.

In addition to a website, there are dozens of other options available, from a business page on Facebook to LinkedIn profiles to an Instagram account to Twitter/X and a blogsite. Small businesses and startups with limited marketing budgets can afford to create free Facebook pages, and Twitter/X or Instagram accounts.

Of course, the more social media apps you use, the more time you need to devote to feeding them by regularly updating the content. So you need to be strategic. What social media channels are most likely used by your ideal client? If you are marketing to millennials and Gen Z, an Instagram account is more likely to be noticed than a Facebook page. For many other businesses, LinkedIn is vital.

How often will you post new content? Many businesses blog monthly or quarterly but do daily posts on platforms like Facebook and Instagram. What if you don't like writing blogs or posting daily on various platforms? No problem.

Outsource the bulk of these tasks to a social media marketing company. It's all a matter of time and money. Where can you best spend your time and how much do you want to spend? Social media consultants are available at a wide variety of price points and expertise. Your only limit is the size of your marketing budget. Be sure to research the vendor's reliability and quality, much as you expect your clients or customers to do with your business.

> As soon as you are financially able to do so, consider outsourcing your web-based marketing to a company (probably another small business) that provides social media services. An outsourced marketer can create social media campaigns to advertise your business and is more likely to be up-to-date on the latest marketing channels since new apps show up every day. Outsource your marketing so you can focus on what you're selling.

Common Risks

Sales and marketing can generate many risks for a small business owner. For example, a company that sells to individual consumers (B to C) rather than to other businesses (B to B) should expect to be accused of violating consumer protection laws. It's a matter of when, not if, such an accusation will be made. The accusation can be based on false advertising. Ever heard the old saw about "buying a pig in a poke"? That adage relates to false advertising. The buyer doesn't know what she or he is buying.

Cam decided to expand her weekend glam experiences to include camping trips. A young couple of novice adventurers ignored Cam's advice to avoid the poison oak patch near their luxury yurt.

The young couple sued Cam's business for false advertising, deceptive business practices, loss of consortium, and intentional infliction of emotional distress. Cam had to put her expansion plans on hold while she paid her attorney to defend the lawsuit. Her children updated their resumes in case they needed to bail on their cushy jobs working for their mom.

Fortunately, Cam had paid her lawyer to create a "disclaimer" to all her clients explaining the risks involved even on a glam campout with luxury yurts. Cam eventually prevailed in court but suffered bad publicity in the local news and a whacking big hole in her bottom line on the way to the win.

Another frequent consumer complaint is the accusation that a business is selling defective products, such as a lawn mower that chops off the user's toes or a blender that blows up while making daiquiris. Companies that sell services to consumers, such as internet providers or home alarm systems, may be accused of shoddy services if the internet connection frequently fails or the alarm system doesn't work as expected. But forgetting your password would not be a design defect of the alarm system's manufacturer.

The sad fact is that a business is unlikely to win in court arguing that the customer was an idiot who misused the product or failed to follow the instruction manual. Consumer protection laws were originally intended to protect even idiot consumers from fraudulent sales practices and clearly unsafe products. While some people believe these laws have become too lopsided in favor of idiots, the laws do protect the end user, a human being, from unsafe practices and products.

> The Ford Pinto car was marketed to consumers as a cute little hatchback that made good gas mileage. The car became infamous for a design flaw which caused the gas tank to explode with lethal force when the car was rear-ended in a traffic accident, even at slower speeds. The Pinto class action lawsuits revolved around how much the company knew about this design flaw but failed to disclose to consumers and government regulators. Pinto cars are now on the slagheap of history.

Thanks to the Pinto car litigation and similar situations, many manufacturers now face "strict liability," meaning the manufacturer will be liable for injuries resulting even from misuse of their product. Consumer protection laws have evolved to protect the end user from harm even when the end user (consumer) exhibits a total lack of common sense. That's why consumer protection laws have expansive definitions.

Tennessee's Consumer Protection Act (TCPA) defines a "consumer" as a natural person (i.e., a living, breathing human) who buys, rents or leases any goods, services, or property including real estate, and "any other article, commodity, or thing of value." As this definition indicates, virtually any sales or marketing activity to *non-businesses* is covered by the consumer protection law.

Another law that all small business owners should be aware of is the Tennessee Personal Rights Protection Act. This law prohibits using another person's image, such as a photo, for commercial purposes without first getting the consent of the photographed or videotaped individual. These days, most people post candid photos on social media platforms such as Twitter/X or Instagram or Facebook during an event or activity. Since these images are not intended for commercial purposes, meaning to make money, there might be no violation of the Tennessee law.

Businesses also take photos at events they sponsor. These photos are often posted on the company's website or on its social media accounts to highlight the company's community involvement and activities. In these instances, the photos are usually not considered commercial because they are not intended to make money for the business.

However, if you have doubts about whether you are complying with the Tennessee law, you might ask everyone in the picture if they consent to you taking their photo. If they say no, then don't take their photograph and certainly don't post in on your company's social media sites or use it in your next marketing brochure. The best practice is to have signed consent forms from everyone and again, don't use their photo if they object. This is one case where it is definitely easier to ask permission first than to seek forgiveness later. Forgiveness could cost a bucket of money.

Cam Flowers likes to take photos of her clients enjoying their adventurous tours. But she always obtains written permission from her clients to use photos of them in her marketing materials.

That has protected her from several threatened lawsuits by adventurers who thought they looked fat in the photos or were too sweaty and disheveled. Cam has learned the hard way that her people want to look glamorous on a glam safari. If they wanted to look hot, sweaty, and exhausted, they'd have their photo taken at their local gym.

HUMAN
RESOURCES

We have arrived at the liveliest and most maddening functional area of any business: the people who work for the company. As a company owner, an HR manager or a compliance officer, you've probably already noticed that most of the compliance issues you face involve employees. That's due to human nature.

Human nature hasn't changed since the first humans got together to kill a wild beast for dinner. Any time two or more humans must work together, something is likely to go wrong. In the modern business world, there will be conflicts between managers and employees and among employees. Your company's HR policies are an attempt to mitigate those risks of conflict.

HR compliance issues are too complex to be covered in detail in this book. A huge industry exists to help companies deal with their HR issues, including industry trade organizations such as the Society for Human Resource Management (SHRM). This book will only highlight some common risks and key laws or regulations that you should be aware of as a small business owner or the compliance person handling HR issues for your small company.

A Word about Culture

Employee relations begin with corporate culture. Every company has a culture which defines how workers and customers will be treated. The culture of many companies is unplanned and unintentional because these aren't the sort of touchy-feely questions most business owners think about when creating a company.

In hindsight, that can be a mistake because your company's culture can be the difference between success and failure, particularly for new companies. New companies usually don't have the finances to compete with larger competitors who can offer employees high wages or generous benefit packages that keep them on the payroll. The trade-off is that new companies usually offer more opportunities for creativity and individual achievement, which employees appreciate.

> How do you see your employees?
>
> As a cost center, forever whining and underperforming?
>
> As an asset, doing the work that makes clients or customers happy so that they continue buying from your business?
>
> What you expect is what you'll get!

Take a moment to think about how your former employers treated their employees. You left them for a reason, after all. Did they view employees as a necessary evil, to be constantly watched for signs of laziness? Did they begrudge every penny spent on their employees? Were benefits skimpy, such as offering so few days of paid time off (PTO) that employees were forced to choose between using their PTO when they or their children were sick or having an actual vacation? Was the company lousy at communicating corporate goals but quick to blame employees when something went wrong?

Or did you work for companies who viewed their employees as the most valuable asset in the business, to be treated with respect and rewarded for hard work? Did these employers support skills training, promoting from within and recognizing employees for showing initiative even when the outcome was an epic failure? Did they have leave policies that allowed employees to take care of their health and spend time with their families?

Both types of employers are examples of a corporate culture. Few business owners begin with a plan to mistreat employees, but they become disillusioned. Employees will never care about your business the way you do because for them, it's just a job. Owners rarely understand how poorly they communicate their goals and expectations for the company. Owners then become frustrated with their employees. The employees become frustrated because they don't know what is expected of them.

> Few business owners begin with a plan to mistreat employees. But many business owners don't realize how poorly they communicate company goals and expectations. As misunderstandings escalate, owners become frustrated with their employees. Employees become frustrated because they don't know what is expected of them. Before long the workplace is toxic.

As you go through this next section on employee relations, think about how your company can create HR policies that support the kind of corporate culture that you want. The best way to keep employees happy and on the payroll is to develop an excellent corporate culture that encourages them to succeed with the company. Think of it as the business version of the Golden Rule.

Pre-Employment Phase

W-2 v. 1099 – Who Am I Hiring?

The first HR issue that most new companies face is deciding whether to hire an employee (W-2 worker) or an independent contractor (1099 worker). Employees are protected by employment laws that set everything from minimum wage rates to employee benefits, such as retirement plans and health insurance. Individual contractors hired as independent contractors are essentially micro-businesses who are generally not covered by the employment law requirements and must pay for their own retirement account and health insurance.

A few employment law requirements do affect the independent contractor relationship. For example, employers have an obligation to protect their employees from sexual harassment by independent contractors. Also, if the independent contractor is itself a small business, its employees will be entitled to workers compensation, unemployment compensation, and other employee protections.

This difference is most dramatically illustrated in how payroll taxes are handled. A W-2 employee splits the 15.3% FICA payroll tax with the employer. But a 1099 independent contractor must pay the full 15.3% FICA payroll tax. An employee is eligible for unemployment insurance if the employee becomes unemployed. An independent contractor is not, except for a brief period during the covid-19 pandemic. As a result, 1099 workers gain a bit of freedom from annoying bosses in exchange for working without the safety net required for W-2 workers.

Obviously, financial bookkeeping is easier for a small employer who decides to classify everyone as an independent contractor because there's no need to figure out the payroll taxes. That is why the most common mistake made by small businesses is to classify a worker as a 1099 rather than a W-2.

That leads to another common mistake: failure to withhold payroll taxes from the worker's pay and submit the withheld taxes quarterly to the IRS. In Tennessee, beginning in 2019, employers must pay state employee taxes, such as contributions to the unemployment insurance fund, every quarter to the Tennessee Department of Labor and Work-force Development (TN Workforce). As a new employer, you must create an employer account using the link on the TN Workforce website.

So before going down the road to payroll tax perdition, small business owners should consider how the IRS and the U.S. Department of Labor (DOL) decide who's a 1099 and who is a W-2. The prevalent test is the "control" test, which is based on the employer's control of how, when, and where the employee works. Under the "control" test, the more control the business exercises over how, when, and where the worker performs assigned tasks, the more likely it is that the worker will be considered a W-2.

> Cam hires another safari guide and requires the guide to work 9 am – 5 pm, Wednesday to Sunday each week. During those hours, the guide creates new tours based on feedback she receives from Cam. Cam pays the guide an hourly wage. Under the control test the guide would most likely be a W-2 employee.
>
> Now imagine that Cam hires another guide to create new safari tours for The Glam Guide's customers. Cam tells the guide she wants a new tour every 6 months and agrees to pay only for tours that attract a pre-set minimum number of adventurers.
>
> The guide creates tours based on her notions of what will sell and then gives the tour guidelines to Cam. The guide works whenever she needs more money to bet on the ponies at the local racetrack. Under the control test the guide would most likely be considered a 1099 independent contractor.

In 2015, the federal Department of Labor's (DOL) Wage and Hour Division (WHD) expressed concern that the "independent contractor" classification was being abused. Their concern arose out of two popular models for outsourcing labor costs.

The first model dates to the 1980's downsizing frenzy caused by the "lean manufacturing" business model, which is a great business model, if a bit cold-blooded toward employees. In this model, some processes were automated or streamlined so that fewer workers were needed. Companies laid off swaths of employees or offered employees early retirement.

Then some of the workers were rehired to do their old jobs but were classified as independent contractors on short-term contracts with no employee benefits. The immediate effect was to dramatically reduce corporate expenses, which flattered the bottom line. Company executives rewarded themselves with bigger pay packages and stock options that were blessed by shareholders who thought management had brilliantly boosted profitability.

> During the 1980's downsizing frenzy, to paraphrase a Jerry Reed country music song.... Management got the gold mine; workers got the shaft.

In recent years, the DOL has focused on the second model for outsourcing, the gig economy. In the gig economy, workers are the business owners, choosing when, where, and how they work. In exchange for scheduling freedom and creative control of their work product, gig workers are paid a set fee and receive no employee benefits. The most common example of this model are the Uber and Lyft drivers. Unfortunately, many quickly find themselves making significantly less than they made as employees.

> The best historical examples of gig workers are actors and musicians, which is why so many of them are talented bar tenders and wait staff at your favorite restaurants.

Since the largest expense for companies is the cost of employee wages and benefits, downsizing and the gig economy flatter a company's bottom line and boost profits. But the flip side is that workers who are classified as independent contractors miss out on employee benefits programs, like a 401(k) retirement plan or group health coverage, and must pay both the employer and employee portions of the payroll taxes.

In response to the perceived abuse of the independent contractor category of workers, the Obama Administration created an "economic realities" test in 2015. The economic realities test looked at whether the worker is economically dependent on the employer based on the totality of circumstances. The DOL cited the following factors:

1. The extent to which the work performed is an integral part of the employer's business.
2. The worker's opportunity to make a profit or loss.
3. The extent of the relative investments of the employer and the worker. How much has the worker invested in facilities and equipment compared to employer?
4. The amount of initiative, judgment or foresight in open market competition with others required for the success of the alleged independent contractor.
5. The degree of independent business organization and operation of the alleged independent contractor.
6. The permanency of the relationship.
7. The degree of control exercised or retained by the employer.

It's easy to see that the new "economic realities" test meant virtually any worker was likely to be re-classified as an employee (W-2) rather than an independent contractor (1099). The new test could have wiped out the gig economy epitomized by companies like Uber, Lyft, and many social media companies that serve small businesses.

Before business owners bought sackcloth and ashes, the 2016 presidential election brought in the Trump administration which announced that it was dropping the economic realities test and creating a new test which emphasized the amount of control. In 2021, the new Biden administration withdrew the Trump administration's rule; but a federal judge reinstated the rule. In response, a new regulation was proposed on October 13, 2022, by the Biden administration and is wending its way through the rule-making process.

The same seven factors listed above were relied on by the Obama, Trump, and Biden administrations when deciding whether a worker is an independent contractor. However, they applied the factors differently. The Obama and Biden administrations favor looking at the totality of the circumstances, while the Trump administration relied almost entirely on the control factor.

In Tennessee, employers should be prepared for the broader interpretation of the economic realities test. Tennessee, along with Kentucky, Michigan, and Ohio, is within the jurisdiction of the U.S. Sixth Circuit Court of Appeals. In 2019, the Sixth Circuit used the economic realities test to decide that off-duty police officers working part-time for a security company were likely to be employees entitled to overtime pay. See, *Acosta v. Off-Duty Police Services Inc.*, 6th Circuit Court of Appeals, Nos. 17-5995/6071 (Feb. 12, 2019).

> When in doubt, it's probably a safer bet to classify workers as W-2 employees and hire a CPA firm that provides payroll services for its small business clients. A CPA firm costs a lot less than IRS (and state) penalties for guessing incorrectly.
>
> You can also ask an employment law attorney for legal advice on whether your workers are W-2's or 1099's. The legal opinion won't be able to give you a "yes" or "no" answer because the IRS "control test" and the DOL "economic realities test don't provide a bright line test. The legal opinion will look at the totality of circumstances to assess whether the IRS and DOL are likely to decide your workers are W-2's or 1099's.
>
> A legal opinion is expensive but still less costly than paying a lawyer to defend your company against IRS and DOL claims of misclassification.

Job Descriptions

It may seem odd to think about job descriptions when you have no employees, but job descriptions fulfill three critical needs for any business.

First, a written job description is the blueprint to help you identify which applicant has the right skills for the job you need to fill. Second, job descriptions allow prospective employees to understand what is expected of them. Third, after an employee is hired, the job description allows you to compare the job duties to the employee's actual performance when you are deciding whether the employee is eligible for a promotion and pay raises.

Another vital function of a job description is to assess whether an employee is able to fulfill their duties. This question usually arises when an employee is hurt on the job. Job descriptions are used by workers compensation doctors to assess whether an employee is able to return to light duty or is no longer able to perform the basic job functions of their pre-injury job. We'll look at workers compensation issues later.

Fitness for duty can also arise in situations where an employee becomes ill with a chronic or terminal illness. At some point in time, the employee may no longer be able to fulfill the requirements of the job description, even with an accommodation as required by the Americans with Disabilities Act (ADA), if this law applies to your company. An up-to-date job description will allow the treating physician to assess whether the employee can continue performing the job duties with an accommodation or the employee is no longer capable of doing the job even with an accommodation.

An up-to-date job description is...

1. A checklist for deciding whether a job candidate has the necessary skills, knowledge, and experience to do the job.
2. A guide for evaluating the employee's job performance.
3. An objective basis for determining whether an employee injured on the job is medically fit to return to work, or an employee with a health condition can continue performing job duties.

The Hiring Process

With a job description hot off the presses, you're ready to hire a new employee. That's when a new set of compliance risks arise.

The most common risks arise from allegations of discrimination based on age, disability, gender, ethnicity, national origin, religion, pregnancy or genetic information. These categories are known as protected classes under Title VII of the Civil Rights Act of 1964. It is illegal under federal law for employers to discriminate against job applicants and employees who are members of these protected classes. Sexual orientation is also now recognized as a protected class in a growing number of states although the federal government's position flipflops depending on which political party controls the White House.

Technically, Title VII of the Civil Rights Act applies only to employers with at least 15 employees, or 20 employees if the allegation relates to age discrimination. Don't be fooled. Every individual of working age knows about these protected classes and expects every employer to comply with the law's requirements.

Small business owners with less than 15 employees tend to voluntarily comply because they believe it is morally right to do so, or they want to avoid the bad publicity of a complaint or they think it's the only way to attract qualified job candidates. So be prepared to comply even if your company has fewer than 15 employees. Remember, you're looking to hire people who have the skills, knowledge, and abilities to do the job and it doesn't matter what gender, race, or other protected status the applicant is.

In addition to Title VII, the federal Americans with Disabilities Act (ADA) prohibits discrimination against individuals with disabilities. The ADA applies to any employer with at least 15 employees. In Tennessee, the Tennessee Human Rights Act (THRA) and Tennessee Disability Act (TDA) generally track the ADA but lower the threshold to a minimum of eight employees.

The next big risk during the hiring process is the misuse of information uncovered during a pre-employment background check. We'll look at these risks in more detail below.

Outsourcing the Hiring Process

Outsourcing the hiring process has tremendous benefits for small companies because the hiring process can be time consuming. Small business owners can save valuable time by hiring a headhunter, recruiter, talent scout, or whatever euphemism is in vogue when your company decides to research outsourcing the process. But small company owners should remember two key risks of outsourcing.

First, employment laws generally hold employers responsible for legal claims based on the hiring process. These legal claims may arise from allegations of negligent hiring, violations of Title VII or violations of laws for conducting pre-employment background checks of job applicants.

This liability doesn't go away simply because the hiring process is outsourced to a recruiting agency. Besides, if you read the fine print closely on your contract with the recruiter, you'll notice that the recruiter requires you to indemnify them if they are sued for actions taken on your behalf. These indemnification clauses are rarely (never in my experience) mutual. So you, the employer, will most likely be on the hook contractually and legally.

Second, this is a collaborative process. Recruiters are only as good as the information they receive from your company. If you lack up-to-date job descriptions which accurately describe what is needed, a recruiter won't be able to screen applicants for what you really want.

Camilla Flowers decided to outsource hiring to a head-hunter agency because she is a creative woman who prefers to not get bogged down in the details. At the request of the headhunter, she jotted down a few notes on the back of an envelope, listing hiring criteria. She wanted a resilient, friendly person who could take clients on glam tours. They had to be high class.

The headhunter sent over blue-haired retirees who had previous museum docent experience. Then she sent over young society debutantes who were bored with their college studies but whose parents wouldn't pay for another year of "study" in Europe.

Cam fired the recruiter and complained to her friends that she'd wasted her money. The recruiter considered changing her profession to pet grooming because animals are easier to work with than people.

Whether your company outsources or handles recruiting in-house, you need to know the basics of employment laws, particularly Title VII. Let's assume your company decides to handle the process in-house and take a closer look at the basics of the hiring process. Remember that we're just skimming the surface of these complicated issues. The goal here is to provide enough information to help you avoid the obvious pitfalls, and to know when to call in the services of a professional HR person or a lawyer.

Employment Ads

Employment ads must comply with federal and state laws that prohibit discrimination against the protected classes. Protected classes include people with disabilities as mentioned above.

Employment ads should track the key job duties in the job description. For example, if a key duty requires the new hire to be able to install

HVAC systems, it would be silly to hire a person who doesn't know a wrench from a screwdriver. Job ads should also list the key physical requirements, such as frequent standing, bending, or lifting. A great example are the FedEx and UPS ads each autumn seeking seasonal employees who must be able to lift 50 pounds.

Job ads also should avoid our unconscious biases. These biases are so ingrained we don't even know they exist, but they can rise up to bite an unsuspecting small business owner. For example, a study found that using words such as "aggressive" tended to deter women from applying for the job even if they were fully qualified based on the job description. Ads saying that the prospective employee must have a clean record may deter people with a criminal record even if their prior conviction would have no effect on their ability to do the job. The moral of the story is to be aware of how bias can affect our choices. The best practice is to use gender neutral adjectives, like "energetic" or "enthusiastic" and to always tie the job ad to the job duties by including bullet points of the key skills or responsibilities copied directly from the job description.

> To avoid unconscious biases, use gender neutral adjectives, like "energetic" or "enthusiastic" and always tie the job ad to the job duties by including bullet points of the key skills or responsibilities copied directly from the job description.

Employment Applications

Employment applications are now a hotly disputed area of employment law, primarily due to questions about salary history and criminal convictions.

Salary history

Asking for an applicant's salary history was traditionally used as a tool in the hiring process. Most job applications included a section where an applicant was supposed to plug in the beginning and ending hourly wage or annual salary for every prior job.

Imagine that your company set a salary range for a position but a job applicant listed a previous salary significantly above what your company can pay. You'd only be human to expect this applicant to use your company as a temporary paycheck until something better paying comes along. Why hire someone who might not be committed to your company for more than a nanosecond? So that application probably gets dumped in the circular file after 30 seconds.

Now imagine how salary histories can discriminate against women and minorities. Historically, women and minorities were paid lower hourly wages and salaries compared to white males doing the same job. Since most companies used a job applicant's salary history as the basis for their own wage or salary offer pay inequities continued and became institutionalized.

> *The Life and Times of Rosie the Riveter* is a 1980 documentary highlighting salary, race and gender inequities during World War II when women did "men's work" in factories to support the war effort.
>
> The women soon learned that black women were paid less than white women and all women were paid substantially less than men for doing the same job. The women were fired the day the war ended in Europe so that they wouldn't "take jobs away from the men."

To address these historical inequities, many states now have laws that prohibit employers from asking about a job applicant's past rate of pay. Tennessee does not have a such a law, as the most recent bill proposed during the 2020 – 2021 session of the state legislature died in committee. However, you might decide to ignore the lack of action by Tennessee for two reasons.

First, as your business expands and you begin hiring employees in other states, you will bump into these laws. The number of states with such laws changes so you will need to do a little research before hiring outside Tennessee. Second, the workforce is shrinking and your company will need to compete for workers. As always, the simplest solution is to set aside the gender or ethnicity of the job candidate and base your wage and salary offers on the individual's knowledge, skills, and experience.

Ban the Box

Another issue with job applications relates to criminal convictions. Historically, a single felony conviction could mean a job applicant was ineligible for hire, without regard to how old the conviction was or what the job duties involved. Clearly no company wants to hire a convicted embezzler as their next chief financial officer and we definitely do not want pedophiles working with children at a day care center or school or church youth group.

But not all felony convictions are alike. The sad fact of life is that minorities, particularly African-Americans, have a proportionately higher rate of criminal convictions. One frequently cited reason is the 1980's "war on drugs" in which convictions for the use or possession of crack cocaine favored by black drug users received significantly harsher prison sentences than convictions for powder cocaine favored by white drug users. Zero tolerance and policing priorities meant more blacks than whites ended up with criminal convictions.

To correct this historical bias, many states now have laws prohibiting employers from asking about criminal convictions in the initial phase of the hiring process. These laws prohibit asking about convictions on the job application. The purpose of these laws is to ensure that an otherwise qualified job candidate is not screened out immediately based on a criminal conviction. These laws vary from state to state.

Tennessee's ban-the-box law applies only to state government, although many private sector employers are voluntarily complying with the law. The law prohibits state government from asking about criminal convictions on the job application. Government employers may ask about criminal convictions later in the hiring process after winnowing down the applicants to those individuals with the required skills, knowledge, and experience.

There is an exception if a person is applying for a "covered position," in which a criminal conviction is an automatically disqualifying event. Covered positions generally refer to jobs at childcare facilities, schools and nursing homes because these employers serve vulnerable populations.

Of course, prohibiting employers from asking about a job applicant's past criminal record left employers wondering how to avoid being sued for negligent hiring or supervision. As a result, employers sometimes opted not to hire minorities, knowing that they were likelier to have criminal backgrounds thanks to the drug war of the 1980's.

In response, a new set of laws are being enacted to help individuals with criminal convictions become employable. These laws generally protect the employer from liability for claims alleging negligent hiring or supervising if the employer follows the process set out in the statute.

The Tennessee version is called the Restoration of Citizenship Act and it provides limited protection for employers from claims of negligent hiring or supervision when they hire employees with prior criminal conviction(s) who obtain a "certificate of employability." These certificates are issued by a court in the county where the criminal conviction originated based on a petition filed by the convicted person.

Few employers have hired based on the Restoration of Citizenship law because the entire compliance burden falls on the person with the criminal conviction. The individual must petition a court in the county where the conviction was handed down, bring character witnesses to a hearing, and pay every conceivable court cost associated with the petition along with any outstanding court fines or fees. The financial burden is cost-prohibitive for most convicted felons who are (wait for it) unemployed. The Tennessee Legislature periodically considers tweaking the law to reduce the financial burden.

Tennessee's newest law on the subject is the Reentry Success Act of 2021. This law says an employer can't be sued for negligent hiring, training, retention or supervision based solely on the fact that an employee has a previous a criminal conviction. There is a limit on the protections for the employer. For example, the employer is not protected if it knew or reasonably should have known that the prior conviction was for a violent crime or a sex crime.

> Cam recently discovered that alternative lifestyle people are just like everyone else. They want a glamourous experience, too. They are often DINK's (dual income, no kids) which allows them to blow their money on themselves.
>
> Cam hires a new guide, Jeff, who has more tattoos than a professional soccer player and a criminal record. Cam doesn't care. Jeff's not going to be engaging in any activities remotely related to the activities that led to his conviction.
>
> Her customers don't care either. Jeff knows all the out-of-the-way places shunned by tourist families with cranky children in tow, he can recommend the best tattoo artists, and he understands all the references to *A Nightmare Before Christmas.*
>
> His criminal conviction gives him street cred with middle class suburbanites who want to experience the wild side of life from a safe and glamorous distance. Cam is so pleased with the results that after six months she gives Jeff a raise.

How long should job applications be held?

Job applications can be used as evidence in claims alleging discrimination for failing to hire an individual based on that individual's protected status or negligent hiring if a new employee harms a co-worker or customer of your business. Since the job application is a key document in such a claim or lawsuit, employers should hang on to these applications. The question is how long should you hang on to them?

If an applicant is not hired, employers have discretion on how long to hold the application. But the employer must tell job candidates at the beginning of the application process. That's why most employers have a notice on their website or on the paper application form specifying how long they will hold the job application. The notice says something like *"Due to the volume of response, we cannot review every application. We hold applications for 30 days [or 60 or 90 days] from the date of submission. Please feel free to re-apply."* Then make sure you follow your stated policy on retaining job applications!

If a job applicant is hired, the general rule is that the job application must be kept in the employee's personnel file for the duration of their employment and for a period of time after employment ends. The time period is usually tied to a statute of limitations for specific types of claims.

The statute of limitations varies, depending on the specific law or type of claim. For example, Title VII of the Civil Rights Act requires an employer to retain the job application for one year from the date the application is received. The Age Discrimination in Employment Act sets a two-year retention period.

Cam's recent announcement that she was hiring caused an avalanche of resumes which clogged her email in-box and her P. O. box. Most of the applicants were absurdly unqualified and Cam decided to get rid of these resumes because she didn't see any point to keeping them.

Cam hired Jeff. Then she notified the few candidates who had been interviewed that the position was filled.

One unsuccessful interviewee, Ashleigh, won't accept a polite thank you for applying but we've filled the position. Cam stopped returning her phone calls after Ashleigh screamed, "it's not fair!" and threatened to file an EEOC complaint against The Glam Guide.

Cam knows that she has less than 15 employees and is technically below the threshold for EEOC jurisdiction. But she decides to prepare anyway. She digs through the "shred" box and pulls out every resume she can find to save them in case the EEOC contacts her.

As a small employer, it is a good idea to keep the job application with the employee's personnel records for three years after the employment relationship ends. This retention period should ensure any applicable statute of limitations expires before your company disposes of the employee's personnel file. Disposing means shredding so that personal information, such as driver's license numbers or social security numbers or birth dates in the file can't be stolen.

Interviewing

After screening all the job applications to weed out those who fail to meet the minimum education or experience requirements, it's time to move to the next phase of the hiring process. You're ready to interview the lucky job candidates.

Most companies start with an initial round of phone interviews. A phone interview might reveal that an applicant has already accepted another job and is no longer available. The phone interview is also an opportunity to assess the applicant's character. Job candidates who sound bored or hostile or rude, who can't remember the details of what's in their resumes or who say they wouldn't be able to work the scheduled hours are probably not going to be a good fit as an employee.

Job candidates who pass the phone interview stage, meaning they are still available and interested in your company's job, are next scheduled for an in-person interview. During the covid pandemic most in-person interviews were conducted via Zoom, Microsoft Teams, or similar services. The good news was that this allowed employers to widen the pool of job applicants to include people who were planning to relocate or who would be able to work remotely.

Interviewing job candidates is fraught with the perils of discrimination because Title VII of the Civil Rights Act applies to the questions you may ask. It is best to use the job description as the basis for your questions and ask only about the individual's ability to perform the job duties and requirements. You will also want to use the same set of questions in each interview so that you can compare responses.

Examples of bad questions include asking a young woman if she's married, has children or is planning to start a family. (Would you ever ask a young man these questions?!) But you could ask her if she would be available to routinely work nights and weekends, if that is a job requirement for everyone in the same or a similar job to the one for which she is interviewing. Don't ask about the job applicant's religion. Do ask if the person would be available to work on a Saturday or Sunday, if that's a job requirement.

> Would you ever ask a young man if he's married, has children, or is planning to start a family? Of course not! So don't ask a young woman these questions.

HUMAN RESOURCES

Interviewing can involve much more than simply asking questions. Some employers use personality tests to assess a prospective employee's "fit." While these tests might be tools for separating the good from the great candidates, they do come with some risks. Recent studies show these personality tests have an inherent bias in favor of white, middle-class applicants. That's not surprising since the tests are designed by people with a similar background.

That's why some employers are focusing more on a demonstration of the skills of the candidates, usually for those job candidates who survive the initial round of interviews. For example, a plumbing company might create a training space where job candidates are required to fix a leak or install a plumbing fixture to prove they have the minimal required skills. A computer tech could be asked to solve a help desk type of problem (and if they can do it, hire them before they get away!).

Background Checks

The phone and in-person interviews will winnow down the job applicants further so that you can begin the next phase which is conducting background checks. At this point in the process, each remaining job applicant should have the education, skills, and experience necessary to do the job. Now you need to verify the applicant's information. Remember that all background checks should be limited to job-related information. Start this due diligence process by verifying the information in the resume.

Resume details

Are the details in the resume accurate and true? For example, did that individual really graduate from Harvard or are they just fluffing their resume? Did they work for NASA or just visit the space center at Huntsville, Alabama on a school trip? Do they hold the licenses or certificates they say they earned and are they in good standing with the licensing authority?

You will want to contact former employers to confirm that the job candidate worked for them, how long they worked for that employer and whether they are eligible for re-hire. Many former employers worry about being sued for defamation if they report anything unflattering about a former employee. Don't be surprised if some former employers will only confirm the date of hire, date of termination, and whether a person is eligible for rehire.

"Eligible for re-hire" indicates many things, even if the former employer won't reveal any gory details. For example, a person not eligible for re-hire might have been fired for cause or they might not have followed the former employer's rule that says failing to give two weeks' notice before quitting makes a person ineligible for rehire. You should weigh these possibilities when making your final decision on who should receive an offer of employment.

The bottom line is that if an individual lies about their basic credentials, their work history, or other important details in their resume, it's safe to assume they will be less than accurate about what they do for your business. Few small businesses can survive the hit to their reputations caused by the dishonesty or unethical behavior of an employee. Look at the context and severity of the inaccurate information and then decide how much risk you want to take with your business's money and reputation.

Personal references

It's important to contact a job applicant's personal references. Obviously, no job applicant will ask their worst enemy to serve as a personal reference, but you still need to check to ensure the information isn't a total fabrication. For example, if a job applicant lacks the current contact information for a reference, would you want to hire that person to do a job that requires paying attention to the details? If three people, such as former co-workers, personal friends or fellow volunteers from a non-profit organization, can't vouch for the job candidate, can this person function as part of a team?

> Job applicants who can't find at least three people, not including their mother, to vouch for their character are probably not going to be a good hire.

Criminal convictions history

As previously mentioned, employers can still conduct criminal background checks of job applicants, and this is the phase of the hiring process when that is usually done. When doing a criminal conviction background check, keep a couple of pointers in mind.

First, consider the length of time that has passed since the date of the conviction. For example, if a person was convicted of a crime years ago but has since held a job and stayed out of the criminal justice system, then the old conviction may not be relevant to their ability to do the job for which they applied.

Second, consider the nature of the offense. Non-violent offenders could be good job candidates depending on the nature of the job duties. But violent offenders, such as murderers, rapists and armed robbers, might never be suitable candidates for any job position due to the risk of workplace violence. And no one wants an embezzler handling company financials.

Madalyn Murray O'Hair, the foul-mouthed founder of the American Atheists, hired David Waters to work at her organization. Waters had already been convicted of violent crimes and theft. He soon began embezzling from AA.

After being fired in 1995 for embezzlement, Waters organized a criminal conspiracy to get revenge by kidnapping and killing Madalyn, her son and her granddaughter. The family were held captive for about a week while their gold coins were pawned, then they were murdered.

To hide the evidence, the bodies were fed through a woodchipper. A third co-conspirator, Danny Fry, was thought to be a weak link and was also murdered. His body was dismembered to delay identification and prevent the authorities from connecting him to Waters.

Years later, Waters and his primary co-conspirator, Gary Karr, were sentenced to life in prison. Waters died in prison in 2003. In 2021, Karr was resentenced in federal court to almost 50 years.

Criminal convictions are also relevant to your company's insurance coverage. Some industries require employees to be "bondable" meaning able to be covered by a fidelity (honesty) bond or insurance policy. Embezzlers and thieves are extremely unlikely to be insurable or bondable; they've already proven they will cause a loss. But other non-violent offenders may be bondable and insurable. If your company hires someone with a previous criminal conviction, ask your insurance agent to confirm with the insurance company that the new hire will be covered by your corporate insurance coverage.

Credit history

Obtaining the credit history of a job applicant used to be standard procedure for many companies. For example, many employers used personal bankruptcy as proof that a potential hire would steal from the company or have poor money management skills that would make them a risk to the company.

But studies have shown that the most common reason individuals file for bankruptcy is the inability to pay a mountain of medical bills. Consider that a heart attack can easily cost $100,000 in medical bills of which at least 20% ($20,000) is the individual's responsibility. Few people have a rainy-day fund of that size, and they end up filing for bankruptcy. Refusing to hire someone who filed for personal bankruptcy can mean punishing them for circumstances beyond their control and for reasons that have nothing to do with their ability to perform the actual job duties.

The Equal Employment Opportunity Commission (EEOC) began studying the use of credit history to assess whether these background checks had a disparate negative effect against women and minorities and as such were discriminatory. The EEOC can't and won't prohibit employers from verifying a potential employee's credit history. But the EEOC coordinates with the Federal Trade Commission (FTC) to reduce the possibility that employers will be able to use credit histories to discriminate. These regulators require employers to follow the rules of the Fair Credit Reporting Act (FCRA) which are stringent because they are designed for banks and consumer financial lenders.

FCRA requires the employer to obtain the written consent from the job applicant before doing a credit check and to provide a copy of the *Summary of Consumer Rights*. The job applicant must be informed of any negative information in the credit report that is used as the basis for not hiring the person. The job applicant must also be given a copy of the consumer report so that she or he can dispute the information in the report with the credit reporting agency who prepared the report.

Due to the stringent process that must be followed and the potential fines for screwing up, most employers choose not to look at the credit history of every job candidate. Instead, employers may choose to look at the credit history of any job candidate handling money for the company, whether in the accounting department or in a retail location, because of the potential risks of loss due to theft. In some cases, this might be a requirement under the company's insurance coverage.

Hiring practices should be reviewed periodically to ensure there are no violations of federal or state employment laws or credit reporting laws. If your company decides to do credit checks, have a clear internal process that explains which jobs require a credit check and why a credit check is necessary.

Employment Offers

After all the interviewing and background checks, you will finally have narrowed down your choices to a couple of candidates. From these finalists you will make a job offer to your preferred candidate and hope the individual accepts so that you don't have to go through the entire arduous process a second time.

Generally, the company owner or HR manager calls the lucky candidate to make a verbal offer of employment. If the offer is accepted, the candidate should be informed that a written offer of employment will be mailed (or these days, emailed) to her or him.

It's important to always confirm the offer of employment in writing because this is the company's opportunity to set out the parameters of employment. The offer letter should contain a summary of the hourly wage or annual salary offered and the start date. It should also state that the offer is conditional and list the conditions. For example, a new hire might be required to pass a pre-employment drug test after accepting a job offer. Another condition is that the employee must successfully meet federal and state requirements to legally work in the U.S.

For senior positions, the offer letter should also spell out any special perks that the prospective hire has negotiated, such as extra vacation time or bonuses for hitting sales targets.

Finally, the offer letter should clearly explain that it is not an employment contract. Tennessee is an "at will" employment state, meaning that employers and employees are free to end the employment relationship at any time. A poorly drafted employment offer letter could accidentally change that relationship. To ensure that your company's offer letters are well drafted, ask an employment law attorney to create the letter for you.

Hiring v. Leasing Employees

After that quick spin through the basics of how to hire employees, you may decide to out-source the whole mess to a professional employment organization (PEO). In a PEO arrangement, your company leases employees from the PEO and pays a monthly fee for each employee. The PEO is the employer and it hires the workers, offers employee benefits like health insurance, issues paychecks to the employees, pays the payroll taxes, and generally assumes legal responsibility for the employees.

Before outsourcing your company's workers to a PEO, take a deeper dive into what a PEO relationship really means. The PEO relationship is based on a contract between your business and the PEO. Check the small print in the contract to verify who is on the hook if the IRS or a state agency comes looking for unpaid payroll taxes.

The IRS offers a certification program to qualify PEO's as a certified professional employer organization (CPEO) in which the PEO agrees to be responsible for payroll tax withholding and reporting. A CPEO designation would mean that your company, which is leasing the employees, is not liable for payment of the payroll taxes. But remember, the employer – PEO relationship is controlled by a contract between these two parties and that contract can alter their responsibilities.

In addition to the contract's terms, most state laws say that the PEO and the company leasing the employees are co-employers. That means your company could be legally on the hook if the PEO fails to perform a legal obligation, like withholding, reporting and paying payroll taxes.

In Tennessee, employers are jointly and severally liable with the PEO for state unemployment insurance premiums. If the PEO doesn't pay Tennessee's unemployment insurance premium tax assessed on each employee, the employer could be forced to pay the tax in order to continue operating in the state.

In the real-life situations in Tennessee where this has happened, the employer's fee to the PEO included the unemployment tax but for a variety of reasons the PEO failed to forward the money to the state. As a result, the employer paid the tax twice; once to the PEO who failed to submit it to the state, and again when the state made a claim against the employer. It is no defense to argue that your monthly lease payment to the PEO included funds to cover all these fees and taxes.

> Camilla Flowers decided to lease employees from Trustus Services, a company she found after Googling "employee leasing services." Trustus had a beautifully decorated office in a suburban strip mall. Their sales patter sounded great, focusing on how they reduce stress for small companies by handling payroll and employee benefits.
>
> Cam was in a hurry and the print in the contract was so tiny, she gave up trying to read the Terms and Conditions in the contract. She only wanted to know how much she had to pay Trustus each month. She signed at the bottom of the contract and wrote the check for the first month's services.
>
> Over a few months, Cam noticed that the quality of employees provided by Trustus was going downhill. Her calls to complain weren't returned. With the help of a magnifying glass, she read the details of the contract and felt faint.
>
> A few months later, Cam received a text message from a friend telling her to turn on the local news. Cam suffered heart palpitations as she watched the president of Trustus Services doing a perp walk after being indicted for tax evasion and embezzlement.

What does this mean for your company? Outsourcing employees to a PEO might still make sense. You simply want to do some research as you would with any other key vendor for your company to verify that the PEO is financially stable, acts ethically, and is able to do what it promises. Ask for references so that you can talk to other small companies that use the PEO's services.

It's also a good idea to ask an employment law attorney to review the PEO's contract before you sign up. The PEO is unlikely to renegotiate their standard contract but at least you'll know what's buried in the small print and can make an informed decision before signing.

After the Employment Offer Phase

Assuming that you decide to hire rather than lease employees from a PEO, you will move to the next phase of employment. It's time to on-board your new hire. Remember that even if you use a PEO, there will be a bit of on-boarding to train the new worker.

After running all the traps on hiring the perfect job candidate, don't forget the paperwork. Tennessee employers are required to report new hires within 20 days of the date of hire. Tennessee created a centralized portal for reporting new hires, including rehires, which can be accessed at www.tennessee.gov/workforce via the "New Hire Reporting" link or directly at http://tnnewhire.com.

The link will connect you with a portal on the website of the Tennessee Department of Human Services (DHS). DHS will compare the new hire's information with its records for individuals receiving public assistance such as TennCare (Medicaid) or Food Stamps. Newly hired individuals who were receiving public assistance may no longer be financially eligible for those programs after getting a job.

DHS also coordinates with the Department of Children's Services (DCS) to collect unpaid child support. If your new hire is behind on child support payments, he (it's almost always the father) may have his wages garnished to catch up the payments. DHS can also issue a "qualified medical child support order" (QMCSO) which requires an employer to add a new hire's underage children to the employer's group health plan thus reducing the number of children receiving TennCare assistance. If your company doesn't offer a group health plan to employees or the new hire isn't eligible for the health plan, then the QMCSO must be returned to DHS stating so.

On-Boarding

On-boarding is generally envisioned as the activities that occur during the initial thirty days of employment. This is the time to complete the conditions set out in the offer letter, such as drug testing the new hire. It is also customary to ask the new hire to review the employee handbook and enroll in the employee benefits programs for which the new hire is eligible. Many small or startup companies don't offer a health plan or a retirement plan because they don't yet have the income stream to do so.

A frequently asked question is whether to require the new hire to sign an employment contract. Before asking an attorney to draft an employment agreement, consider a few pros and cons. An employment contract alters the "at will" employment status in Tennessee. If not carefully drafted, an employment contract might require you to keep an unsatisfactory employee on the payroll until the employment contract expires.

Employment contracts can be a sensible precaution for senior management people or employees with specialized knowledge needed to run your business. But employment contracts are too often used as a substitute for a non-competition agreement to prevent an employee from working in the same industry, even when the employee doesn't know any of your company secrets or proprietary processes. That is precisely why Tennessee courts tend to dislike employment contracts, viewing them as a restraint on trade.

Before falling in love with the notion of an employment contract for every new hire talk to an employment law attorney about the pros and cons of these agreements. You might be able to mitigate your business risks without an employment contract.

Verifying Eligibility for Employment

A critical hiring step is verifying that the prospective employee is eligible to work in the U.S. The federal requirements are overseen by the U.S. Citizenship and Immigration Services (USCIS). Under federal law, USCIS Form I-9 must be completed for each new hire. The completed Form I-9 must be saved by the employer in the new hire's personnel file but in a folder that is separate from other information in the personnel file. The I-9 must also be retained for three years from the date of hire or for one year after employment ends, whichever time period is longer.

> Always confirm that you are using the current version of Form I-9 by looking at the upper right corner of the first page where it says "Expires [date]". If the expiration date has come and gone, go to https://www.uscis.gov/i-9 for the current version. USCIS can assess a cash fine against companies using an outdated version of the I-9.

USCIS also manages the e-Verify system which is used to verify an individual's eligibility to work in the U.S. Employers need to create an employer account at www.e-verify.gov or www.uscis.gov and then follow the on-line directions for submitting the new employee's social security number for verification.

The e-Verify system automatically compares the individual's name with the social security number to confirm that the identification is valid allowing the individual to lawfully work in the U.S. If the number doesn't match, the *employee* has a limited time period in which to provide documentation to the USCIS to fix the error. Most errors are the result of typos or different spellings of names, a particular problem for people of Hispanic or Middle Eastern heritage.

Cam Flowers decides to expand her business into the local Hispanic community. She hires JP Gomez, whose full name is Juan Pablo Gomez Martinez. Gomez is his father's last name and Martinez is his mother's family name. Adding a mother's family name is common in Hispanic cultures.

When JP went to college a few years back, he anglicized his name to JP Gomez to avoid the usual confusion about his surname. When Cam plugs in JP's name and social security number, the e-Verify system says they don't match and so he can't legally work in the U.S.

JP frantically digs through old records and finds that when his parents applied for a social security number for him, the clerk typed in his surname as Martinez rather than Gomez. After several gut wrenching and agonizing discussions with USCIS, JP proves that he can lawfully work in the U.S.

In Tennessee all employers must complete the Form I-9 on all new hires. In addition, employers with at least 35 employees are required to use the e-Verify system to verify the employment status of new hires. Tennessee law limits an employer's liability when the e-Verify system verifies an employee as "legal" but the Tennessee Department of Labor and Workforce Development later determines the employee is not legally authorized to work in the U.S.

Every employer in Tennessee is required to complete a federal Form I-9 for each new hire. Employers with 35 or more employees must also use the e-Verify system to verify that a new hire may legally work in the U.S.

Salaries and Wages

The Fair Labor Standards Act (FLSA) is the basis for every payroll system in use because it sets a minimum wage, establishes the "workweek," and tells us who is eligible for overtime pay.

A workweek is a period of seven consecutive days. Most employers set their workweek to run from Monday at 12:00 am through Sunday at 11:59 pm. Within that seven-day period, employees may work an 8-hour workday for five days, or a 10-hour workday for four days, or some other variation that adds up to 40 hours during that workweek.

When employees work more than 40 hours in a workweek, they might be eligible for overtime pay. Overtime is calculated as one and one-half times the worker's regular rate of pay. Overtime is paid to non-exempt employees, often called hourly workers.

Hourly workers generally don't have special certifications and don't have supervisory responsibilities. They show up, do their jobs, and then go home. Hourly workers must accurately track their time while at work to ensure they are paid time and a half if they work more than 40 hours in the workweek.

> Hourly workers who work more than 40 hours in a workweek must be paid time and a half for the excess hours. Even if the overtime was not authorized. That's why your company's employee handbook should require all overtime to be approved in advance.
>
> If the employee works unauthorized overtime, your company must pay the overtime pay. But the employee can be counseled for failing to follow the company's policy to get advance approval of the overtime.

Exempt employees, often called salaried workers, are usually not eligible for overtime pay. Their wages are based on an annual amount divided equally into the number of pay periods during the year. To be exempt from overtime, salaried employees must meet both an income test and a duties test.

The income test requires that they must be paid at least $684 per week or $35,568 annually. The duties test generally requires that the employee has supervisory authority over other employees, is a decision-maker for the company or has a job requiring professional degrees and certifications that allow them to exercise independent judgment. Salaried workers who don't meet the salary and duties tests are eligible for overtime.

Minimum wage is a current hot topic. The federal minimum wage was last raised in 2009 to $7.25 per hour. Many states have set a higher minimum wage for workers in their states. In addition, many larger cities are setting a higher minimum wage for workers within their jurisdiction. In these states and cities, the minimum wage is $12 an hour or $15 an hour.

Since the covid-19 pandemic, restaurants, gas stations, grocery stores, department stores, motels and hotels, and similar industries seeking "unskilled" labor are facing significant challenges finding anyone willing to work for them. Some job seekers have traded up to higher paying jobs with better (comparatively) working conditions or retired or simply quit looking for a job. To entice workers to fill these traditionally minimum wage jobs, employers are offering starting wages ranging from $12 to $25 an hour.

Tennessee follows the federal minimum wage rather than having a state-specific law. In response to national and local campaigns to set the minimum wage at $15 an hour, several cities, including Metro Davidson County (Nashville) and Memphis, debated local ordinances adopting $15 an hour as the minimum wage.

That spurred the Tennessee legislature to pass a law prohibiting local governments from enacting ordinances that would require private employers to pay a minimum wage higher than the federal minimum wage. This new law is codified at TCA §50-2-112. However, the new law can best be described as political theater because in the post-covid labor market, many private sector employers have discovered they need to offer a starting rate of at least $12 or $15 per hour in hopes of attracting workers. In 2022, many downtown Nashville restaurants offered starting wages of $18 per hour but still had trouble finding workers willing to put up with sky-high parking rates and swarms of drunken patrons. Inconceivable!

In Tennessee, employers may set a pay period that is one month (12 pay periods per year), every two weeks (26 pay periods), twice a month (24 pay periods) or every week (52 pay periods). Weekly pay periods are common in construction and other blue-collar industries. White collar businesses, such as engineering firms, accounting firms, and tech companies often pay every two weeks. It doesn't matter which method your company uses as long as you are consistent.

On-Going Employment

Put it in Writing

Written policies are not a blunt instrument to be used for beating your employees into submission. Written policies are a tool for educating employees about the company's culture and helping them understand what is expected of them as employees. The policies are also a tool for employees to use when assessing your company's value as an employer.

If your company's HR policies are designed to instill fear and loathing, your employees will live down to your worst expectations before fleeing to greener pastures. On the other hand, if your company's policies emphasize coaching employees about expectations so that everyone can be successful, employees will commit to performances that exceed your wildest dreams.

The most important written policy is the employee handbook. It is the primary source for your company's corporate culture. The employee handbook contains the most important employee policies, from non-discrimination to progressive discipline to the business's operating hours to the timing of performance reviews.

The employee handbook also summarizes the company's leave

policies, such as vacation or sick leave or paid time off (PTO). The employee handbook usually contains a summary of employee benefits like the group health plan and the 401(k) retirement plan, if these benefits are offered. Of course, many small businesses might not have the cash-flow to offer employee benefits until after a couple of years in business.

Camilla Flowers never bothered creating written policies because she trusted her employees and didn't want to stunt their creative ideas. Then she hired Don.

Don misses at least one day a week, leaving customers stranded in unglamorous places, like shopping mall parking lots. His co-workers hate his guts because they must cover for him, ruining their days off.

Recently, Cam met with Don to discuss his poor attendance. Don replied that no one ever told him there was a problem. Cam reminded him of all the staff meetings when they discussed each employee's schedule to ensure all tours were properly staffed. Then Don demanded to know where it's written down that he has to show up on a regular basis. His arrogant, entitled attitude infuriated Cam and she fired him for insubordination. Don screamed "I'll sue!" as he was dragged to the door by his co-workers.

Now Don's suing for wrongful termination and Cam is done trusting her employees. She's planning to create written policies if she has any money left after paying her lawyer to defend Don's lawsuit.

In Tennessee, employers have wide-ranging discretion on employee conditions. Employers are free to pay, or not to pay, for holidays, vacation leave, sick leave, or PTO. Of course, any employer who refuses to pay for these perks will quickly learn that no one will work for a company that offers only the absolute minimum required by law.

Written employee policies can mitigate the risk of misunderstanding between the employer and the employee. However, written policies can be the quickest route to trouble if the company's representative, such as an HR person or a manager, ignores them or enforces them unevenly. Once you put your company's policies in writing, you must follow them.

Assessing Performances

Every employee wants feedback on their performance and to be rewarded for their hard work. But the methods for delivering that feedback have evolved. Baby Boomers resigned themselves to undergoing the dreariness and dread of the once-a-year annual performance review. No one liked this process, not the supervisor filling out the overly long template with numerical scores and boxes for comments, nor the employees who waited a whole year to learn if their wish for a raise or a promotion would be granted.

About twenty years ago, some companies experimented with the 360-review. In this model, the supervisor completed a review of each one of her or his reports. The kicker was that employees had the opportunity to grade their supervisors. Managers don't like being told they have deficiencies any better than their subordinates like hearing such constructive criticism. Not surprisingly, few employers still use this model.

The current models of performance evaluations fall into two general categories. Younger workers, like Millennials and Gen Z, want constant feedback on their performance. Some older workers may interpret this as evidence of insecurity, but this model allows for constant adjustments to improve performance.

The other model calls for monthly or quarterly coaching sessions. In this model, a manager meets with each direct report to discuss the employee's performance and to focus on specific actions for improving performance. The goal is to ensure the employee has the training and tools needed to successfully do their job. This method also allows for a quick intervention if an employee is struggling or isn't a good fit with the corporate culture.

The method your company adopts will probably depend on your attitude toward your employees. As noted earlier, some companies view employees as a cost center to be closely monitored for slacking on the job and generally aren't interested in coaching employees for success. Other companies view employees as their most valuable assets and are adopting a coaching model. Employees who feel valued will always be top performers.

> Herb Kelleher built Southwest Airlines into one of the most successful American businesses on the principle that "happy workers means that your company will have happy customers which will lead to happy shareholders."

WORKING
CONDITIONS

Social Media Risks & BYOD

One of the newer risks facing employers revolves around social media. What if disgruntled employees say derogatory things about the company on social media? What if a group of employees bullies another employee through their personal social media accounts? Should it matter to your company that the employees make their comments from their personal devices outside of regular business hours?

Answers to these questions require balancing an employee's right to personal privacy with the company's desire to protect its reputation and its proprietary information and to enforce its HR policies.

Employers generally have the right to enforce their HR policies against an employee for actions taken outside of the workplace. For example, your employee handbook should have a policy prohibiting discrimination based on a "protected class" under Title VII. So, if your company becomes aware that a group of employees are bullying a co-worker on social media, your company can take action against the employees who violated that policy.

On the other hand, you might have limited recourse if a group of employees trashes your company on social media for having a toxic workplace or lousy employee benefits or for paying less than competitors. That's because these comments may be "protected activities" under the National Labor Relations Act.

In March 2015, the National Labor Relations Board (NLRB) issued guidance that employees have the right to criticize, in person or via social media, their employers, their working conditions, and their wages because all of these activities are "protected activities" under the National Labor Relations Act. Employees can even make false or derogatory statements about their employers so long as the false statements are not "malicious."

This guidance has been modified, but "protected activities" still applies to comments involving wages or working conditions. That said, it does not protect employees engaged in bullying, threatening, or defaming co-workers, employers, or customers. Employees who use social media to violate your company's policies on anti-discrimination or bullying won't get any help from the NLRB.

Cam liked her employees and was always happy to connect with them on social media. Her employees posted photos of company retreats where employees were rewarded for their hard work. They also posted images of glamorous tours with customers creating buzz to draw future customers.

Recently, a Facebook post by long-time employee, Morgan, included a comment from new hire, Taylor. Taylor sneered that the glam tour wasn't as glamorous as her trip to Paris, France, a gift from her parents when she graduated from college with a degree in marketing. Taylor also whined that she had not received a pay raise after 6 months on the job.

Cam was infuriated. She recalled that Taylor played on her cell phone during staff meetings when new tours were planned. Several customers had noted that Taylor seemed bored and disinterested in helping them achieve their shopping nirvana on a glam tour.

The next day, Cam called Taylor into her office and fired her for poor performance. A few hours later, Taylor's daddy called Cam to demand what the hell she meant by firing his little princess who had a legal right to complain about crappy working conditions. After that, Cam called her lawyer to ask if she had done the right thing firing the whiny [deleted since this is a family-friendly book].

In Tennessee, the Employee Online Privacy Act prohibits employers from requiring job applicants or employees to provide passwords to their personal internet accounts or forcing employees to access their personal accounts in the presence of the employer. However, there are important exceptions. One exception is when the employer is investigating employee misconduct that violates an HR policy.

Employers can also request personal passwords for any electronic device (phones, laptops or iPads) that the employer provides for the employee's business use. The employer can also control access to websites on company-provided devices and monitor or block communications on company-owned devices.

Many employees now use their personal devices for business, even if they are only reading their business emails on their personal phones. To spell out the employee's privacy rights and the company's interests in protecting company information, employers should have a BYOD (Bring Your Own Device) policy.

A BYOD policy spells out how and when employees can use their personal devices, like iPads and cell phones, for company business. It also explains that the employer has a right to protect company property, including information about back-office processes and customer information. At a minimum, an employer needs a "kill" switch to cut off access to company systems if an employee's device is stolen or lost and when an employee leaves the company.

One final note on employees accessing work emails on their personal devices. If the employee is a non-exempt employee, they might inadvertently end up working more than 40 hours a week. That means they will be owed overtime pay. Convenience is great but you'll need to include a statement in your employee handbook or in a BYOD policy that reminds employees to "stop working outside of their regularly scheduled hours."

A BYOD policy explains how the company will protect its proprietary information when an employee is using the employee's personal cell phone or other electronic device for business.

But this convenience has a cost. Hourly workers may inadvertently work more than 40 hours a week if they are obsessively responding to work emails outside their regularly scheduled work hours. That means they will be owed overtime pay for the hours exceeding 40 hours in the workweek.

Social Protests in the Workplace

The U.S. is undergoing profound demographic and social changes. By the 2030's, the country will be ethnically and racially more diverse. A shrinking pool of working-age adults will be supporting more retirees. The workforce has already been permanently reduced due to the on-going retirement of Baby Boomers.

To make up for a lack of workers, employers are automating more processes leading to the elimination of entire job classifications. Many older workers wonder if their jobs will be automated away, leaving them little time to learn new skills or build a new career path.

These social changes are happening as the wealth gap is widening with the rich getting richer and the middle class getting squeezed. Many people, including many middle-class workers, feel left behind by globalization with stagnant wages, rising inflation, and fewer opportunities for advancement. As a result, workplace dissatisfaction is increasing.

None of these problems can be or should be fixed by employers. But employers need to accept that it is becoming impossible to keep the culture wars out of the workplace. Employers need a plan to address these issues.

Racial Justice and Discrimination

On May 25, 2020, Floyd George died after almost ten minutes of being slowly suffocated during his arrest by the police. His death was subsequently ruled to be a murder. Several other high-profile deaths of black Americans at the hands of police officers unleashed the Black Lives Matter (BLM) movement. BLM is a political and social movement protesting police brutality and, more generally, racial violence against black people. Hispanic Americans and Native Americans have similar tales to tell.

Employers can't fix social and political ills that go back more than 200 years. However, business owners can control how they treat their employees and customers. That means creating and enforcing anti-discrimination, anti-harassment and anti-bullying policies. It also means ensuring that compensation is based on skills and experience rather than skin color or any other irrelevant status.

Sexual Harassment and the #MeToo Movement

In 2018, the #MeToo Movement used a Hollywood sex scandal involving Harvey Weinstein as the catalyst for demanding a change in how employers (and society generally) handles sexual harassment allegations. Historically, women who alleged they had been sexually harassed by a co-worker were disbelieved, ignored, or pressured to drop their complaint, particularly if they were accusing a higher ranking, C-suite level manager.

> The "Mad Men" television series illustrated many of the same gender discrimination issues that underpin the #MeToo movement.

The movement engendered a backlash as fears grew that it had become a witch hunt against men. But it has also encouraged private employers and government employers to reconsider sexual harassment policies. The EEOC has issued new guidance on sexual harassment training and many employers are enhancing their in-house training.

Some states have passed laws requiring employers to hold annual employee training on sexual harassment. Tennessee does not have a law requiring sexual harassment training and is unlikely to do so any time soon. Despite the lack of a specific legal requirement, Tennessee employers might want to consider following the national trends on sexual harassment training as a way to enhance their ability to recruit and retain employees in a tight labor market.

Aside from training, employers should be aware of a couple of new laws regarding sexual harassment claims and non-disclosure agreements. At the federal level, the Speak Out Act limits the enforceability of non-disclosure agreements (NDA) that include future claims of sexual harassment. In addition, Tennessee has a law that prohibits employers from including sexual harassment claims in a non-disclosure agreement.

Diversity, Equality, and Inclusion (DEI)

Most of the social and political movements have coalesced into a renewed interest in creating more diverse workplaces. Women are still paid less than male colleagues when performing the same jobs; minorities still tend to be the last hired, first fired. In addition to these traditional Title VII protected classes, diversity has expanded to include LGBTQ and gender identification.

In 2015, the U.S. Supreme Court struck down state laws prohibiting same-sex marriages. As a result, employers expanded the definition of "spouse" in their employee handbooks and employee benefits programs to include same-sex couples. Since then, the EEOC has issued guidance expanding the Title VII protections to include lesbian, gay, bisexual, and transgender (LGBT) individuals.

While all that might sound utopian or touchy-feely, remember that millennials and Gen Z people take a more relaxed attitude toward race, ethnicity and gender identity. They are also motivated by causes, including a desire to correct the social injustices that they perceive around them. As a result, adopting HR practices that acknowledge the changing demography of America will ensure your company has an edge over competitors in attracting workers and customers.

Workplace Violence Policies

In 2021, the U.S. averaged one mass shooting per day according to some calculations, although an accurate assessment is impossible since federal and state laws prohibit the gathering of statistics on gun violence.

> According to the Mass Shooting Tracker there were 329 mass shootings (defined as four or more people shot in a single shooting spree) in the U.S. from January 1, 2023, to May 31, 2023.

Many of these mass shootings happen at or near a workplace, including schools. As a business owner, an HR manager or a compliance officer, you need to be aware of the risk that "it couldn't happen here" will prove a false hope.

Workplace violence has many causes, ranging from domestic violence attacks against an employee by an abusive family member, to angry employees enraged they were disciplined or fired for poor performance, to attacks against racial or religious minorities. Underlying many of these attacks are angry individuals, usually white males in their 20's and 30's, who feel cut adrift by the social and economic changes in the U.S.

The threat of workplace violence has increased due to many states loosening their gun ownership laws. Simultaneously, the covid pandemic lockdowns left many individuals feeling isolated and depressed while limiting opportunities for mental health counseling. As a result, the post-covid world seems to be full of anxious, depressed and angry people with easy access to guns. Many employers are now adding "active shooter" training for their employees to increase the chances that most employees will survive if the unexpected happens. They are also reviewing their workplace violence policies.

In Tennessee, employers must balance workplace violence policies with the state's loose gun laws. In 2013, Tennessee enacted a "guns in parking lots" law which allows employees with gun permits to bring their legally owned guns to work, so long as the guns are locked in the permit holder's privately owned vehicle in the parking lot and the gun is not visible to anyone walking by or standing near the vehicle.

Under this law, employers cannot be held civilly liable for damages, injuries, or death arising out of another's actions involving the weapon. Employers did not find the limited liability a comfort and they also found the law confusing. For example, the "guns in parking lots" law appeared to contradict a separate state law (TCA §39-17-1359) that allows employers to post a sign prohibiting guns on their property.

In response, the Tennessee Attorney General issued an opinion (TN Atty. Gen. Op. 13-41) on May 28, 2013, saying the "guns in parking lots" law does not affect the employer-employee relationship and an employer may terminate an employee who brings a gun onto the employer's property (other than a parking lot).

But in March 2015, Tennessee enacted another law that prohibits employers from taking any adverse employment action, including termination of employment, against an employee *solely* because the employee brings a gun to work as allowed by the "guns in parking lots" law. This new law also says that allowing employees to bring guns to work is not proof the employer failed to provide a safe workplace, which may be cold comfort to employers facing wrongful death lawsuits alleging the employer was negligent in hiring or supervising a person who gets his legally-owned firearm from his pickup truck in the parking lot and turns the workplace into a mass shooting event.

In July 2021, Tennessee allowed individuals to own handguns without having a permit ("permitless carry"). Although not explicitly addressed in the new law, it appears that employers can still prohibit employees from bringing their guns into the actual workplace.

It will be extremely difficult for you as a company owner, HR manager, or compliance person to balance employees' expectations of a safe workplace with Tennessee's loose gun laws and our society's generally litigious attitude. It might also be prudent to talk to a lawyer about your legal options for complying with state gun laws while also mitigating the risk of workplace violence.

Workers Compensation

Workers compensation claims arise when an employee is hurt while performing duties or activities "within the scope of employment". On-the-job injuries can happen even with the best safety protocols in place because stuff happens.

Workers compensation laws are designed to create a trade-off for employers and employees. The employee receives lost pay ("wage replacement" in workers comp lingo) and medical treatment for the on-the-job injury in exchange for not suing for additional claims, such as pain and suffering. The employer is obligated to pay for workers compensation insurance coverage for its employees in exchange for limited liability for additional claims related to the injury.

Few people like the workers compensation system. Employers often believe that employees recovering from an injury are simply malingering. Employees think they are being forced back to work before they have recovered. They also believe the monetary compensation for their injuries, including lost limbs, is stingy. (It is.) But it's a workplace reality, so everyone needs to be prepared to follow the process when an injury occurs.

First of all, the injured worker is required to promptly report the injury to the company person designated to take these reports, such as a supervisor, or the HR manager or the company owner. The next step is determining the seriousness of the injury. Does the employee need a Band-Aid for a small cut or an ambulance ride to the nearest emergency room? After determining the severity of the injury, the next step is deciding if the injury is a "reportable" injury.

A reportable injury requires two reports. First, injuries needing more than first aid need to be reported to the company's workers compensation insurance company. The insurance company will then handle the claim. Serious injuries must be reported to both the federal OSHA and the state version of OSHA so that they can conduct an accident investigation. A serious injury is one involving a loss of a limb or a death.

In Tennessee, that means reporting to both the federal Occupational Safety and Health Administration (OSHA) and the Tennessee Occupational Safety and Health Administration (TOSHA). Both agencies have authority to investigate worksites where a serious injury or illness has occurred.

Second, a reportable injury must be listed on the company's Form 300, a standardized injury reporting form. Each year companies with 10 or more employees must also report serious injuries or illnesses on the OSHA Form 300 report. More details about this form and its reporting requirements can be found at www.osha.gov.

Eventually, the injured employee will recover sufficiently so that the process moves to the next phase, the return-to-work phase. At this point, the workers compensation claim revolves around questions of (1) whether the employee is able to do the basic duties and activities of a specific job and (2) when the employee can return to work. The answers to these questions depend on the severity of the injuries.

Workers compensation laws create classifications of injuries, based on the severity of the injury. Classification terms include temporary impairments, partial impairments, permanent impairments and maximum medical improvement or MMI. The level of impairment and improvement will determine the ultimate level of compensation for the injury.

> Cam schedules an annual staff retreat in hopes employees will brainstorm new ideas of how to handle obnoxious customers, like drunken bridesmaids and grown-ups who never heard the word "no" from their parents.
>
> During the lunch break, Wesley decides to demonstrate the touchdown celebration of his favorite NFL player to all his disinterested co-workers. He begins hopping around the room waving his arms like he's in training with Navy semaphore flags, knocking over water bottles and trouncing on toes.
>
> His wild dance ends with a leap. Unfortunately, the room is much smaller than an end zone. His long legs catch on a chair and he drops in a heap with a twisted ankle.
>
> Wesley demands that workers comp pay his medical bills because the accident happened during an activity required by his employer. Cam secretly thinks he's an idiot for wanting to report an injury caused by his own stupidity. But she reports the claim to the workers comp carrier.

Most employees are able to return to work, even if they can't do all the requirements of the job they held at the time they were injured. If the employee is temporarily limited, workers compensation laws require that the employee be offered "light duty" or less strenuous work while the employee continues to recover.

More severe injuries might mean that the employee must undergo training for a new job. In these cases, the employee is sent to a vocational rehabilitation (voc rehab) facility for an assessment of their skills so that they can be encouraged to train for jobs within their new skill level. Severely injured or disabled employees who can't do their old jobs and don't have the education or skills to work at other jobs may apply to the Social Security Administration for disability benefits.

Along this entire journey, the claim and final settlement based on the level of impairment will be handled by the workers compensation carrier. Employers may fume about the length of time before the employee is able to return to work and the claim can be closed. Employers may also fume about the fact that workers compensation premiums are calculated based on a three-year rolling period. That means that an injury this year will remain part of the premium calculations for three years before rolling off the "experience module or mod".

Workers compensation premiums are based on the frequency and severity of each employer's claims. The more claims a company has, the higher the premium charged. The insurer might suggest that the employer require additional safety training with a goal of reducing the frequency of claims. An insurer might even decide to not renew coverage.

To reduce your blood pressure as a company owner, HR manager or compliance officer, consider prudent measures that can limit the "frequency and severity" of workers compensation claims. First, make safety an important part of your company's in-house training. Second, have an up-to-date written job description so that the workers comp doctor can easily assess the employee's ability to return to work. Outdated or non-existent job descriptions are a major handicap to settling workers compensation claims.

A POST COVID WORKPLACE

Covid-19 Pandemic

In January 2020, news stories began mentioning a deadly coronavirus named SARS-CoV-2 that caused high fever and, in the worst cases, respiratory failure and death. Public health systems were quickly overwhelmed as a modern-day Black Plague spread death around the globe. Within months, the global supply chain had seized up as countries went into lockdowns in hopes of slowing the spread of the virus.

In March 2020, many cities and states in the U.S. began imposing public health quarantine orders. The economy ground to a halt as businesses shut in compliance with shelter-in-place laws and ordinances. Only essential businesses, such as hospitals, gas stations and grocery stores, remained open.

On March 18, 2020, Congress passed the Families First Coronavirus Response Act (FFCRA). The law applied to employers with 1 – 499 employees and had two major parts. The first part required employers to offer paid sick leave to employees who had covid-related illnesses or were caring for a family member with covid. The second part required employers to offer paid time off to parents who were unable to work, even virtually, due to a lack of childcare while schools and daycares were closed. The FFCRA expired by October 2021. Although this law is now gone, it set a precedent of paid sick leave.

Covid-related disaster relief laws enacted by the states will continue to be in effect because they usually cover more than just the covid pandemic. An example is the Tennessee Business Fairness Act (TCA §58-2-301 & 302) which provides limited liability to businesses during a natural disaster, including a pandemic, if they follow the safety guidelines set by the governor's office or a state agency. Tennessee employers should be aware that the governor's guidelines during covid often conflicted with the federal guidelines, a situation that could happen again in the next disaster.

Although the federal covid relief law has expired, the effects of covid continue to reverberate in the workplace. The way we work has changed permanently.

The Great Resignation

In the aftermath of the covid pandemic, millions of employees assessed their financial situation and their personal values and resigned from their old jobs. Many Baby Boomers took early retirement, which has permanently shrunk the pool of available workers.

Employees who worked in essential businesses that had remained open during the lockdowns succumbed to burnout. Some employees were cast adrift when their employers succumbed to the financial losses caused by federal and state covid lockdowns and customers switching to internet-based buying.

Of the employees who resigned, 69% had a new job lined up, according to a survey by the Society for Human Resources Management (SHRM). Many of these employees said they were trading in their old jobs for new jobs with higher pay, better working conditions or better benefits.

The great resignation is a mixed blessing for smaller businesses. On the one hand, a shrinking pool of available workers and rising inflation mean businesses need to offer a higher rate of pay to hang on to current employees and to entice new people to accept an employment offer. On the other hand, many employees like the fact that smaller businesses have less bureaucracy and often offer employees more autonomy on how they do their jobs.

Virtual Offices

The covid pandemic also permanently changed the workplace. Prior to the pandemic, companies expected their employees to show up at the office to be closely monitored by their supervisors to ensure no one goofed off on the company dime.

During the covid lockdowns, employees were forced to stay home unless they were essential workers, such as hospital staff or grocery store employees. Companies quickly switched to having employees do their jobs remotely, working from home.

Employees liked working from home because they avoided the aggravation of their daily commutes and enjoyed greater autonomy of how and when they performed their assigned duties. Many companies realized that remote work could serve corporate purposes because it allowed them to reduce overhead costs by renting less office space.

As the pandemic fades into memory, companies and employees are reassessing. Some companies have gone totally virtual with their employees. This allows them to recruit nationally to fill open positions and they can attract workers who have difficulty working a traditional 9 to 5 job, such as mothers of preschoolers or some disabled workers.

Many employers are experimenting with a hybrid model, which combines on-site and remote working. This allows time to build camaraderie among the employees while reducing the number of times they need to commute each week.

An increasing number of employers are demanding that employees return to the office full time. One reason for on-site working is that it facilitates training new hires, particularly younger employees, by providing more interaction with experienced older workers. But the main reason seems to be that these companies are run by owners and managers who grew up in a business world where face time mattered. It's the only way they feel comfortable doing business.

Companies that insist on face time might have trouble recruiting workers in the long run, particularly if their competitors offer all virtual or a hybrid model. Many younger workers seem to prefer remote work, even though they also crave constant feedback on their performance.

Whatever model your business chooses, there are a couple of points to keep in mind. Small businesses need to keep their overhead costs low by limiting the amount of office space they rent. They also need to attract employees. As a result, a remote workforce might work best for them.

Another consideration is how to monitor your workers to ensure that your company complies with applicable employment laws. For example, non-exempt (hourly) workers might be owed overtime pay if they work more than 40 hours during the workweek. These workers need to correctly report their time to ensure the Fair Labor Standards Act (FLSA) is followed. There are many FLSA-compliant electronic timeclocks to track time and attendance. Find the one that integrates most efficiently with your company's payroll system.

Some companies have decided to use cloud-based applications that allow them to track when employees have accessed company databases, including the keystrokes on each employee's computer. This allows the employer to monitor work hours by each employee to limit unauthorized overtime. However, these applications are a surveillance tool which is sometimes abused to micromanage employees. Nobody likes to be spied on.

> A productive workplace like any other relationship depends on trust. Spying on your workers by monitoring when they access a company database and how long they work in the database might sound like a nifty efficiency tool. But ultimately it is more likely to destroy trust and cause employee turnover, which will raise overhead costs as your company must constantly recruit and train new workers.

Employees who know they are being spied on or whose employer doesn't allow them to do their jobs remotely will probably quit and go in search of greener pastures. In a tight labor market, allowing remote work and trusting your employees to do their jobs will enhance your company's chances of hiring and retaining workers.

On the Horizon

Paid Sick Leave

The covid pandemic drew attention to the lack of paid sick leave among small employers. Many small businesses hesitate to offer paid sick leave because it adds an administrative wrinkle to their payroll reporting and because of the financial burden of paying workers to not work.

The pandemic also highlighted the lack of consistency in paid sick leave laws across cities and states. Some states and cities had already passed laws requiring employers to offer paid sick leave. These laws vary significantly from city to city, even in the same state. As a result, employers who operate in more than one state are encouraging Congress to enact a federal law on paid sick leave so that there is a common standard that will make compliance easier for employers.

The paid sick leave movement has not yet reached Tennessee. However, if your company has employees and work sites outside of Tennessee, you will need to comply with the local laws on paid sick leave for the workers in those jurisdictions. Rather than having different rules for different worksites, it might be simpler to standardize your company's HR practices by offering paid sick leave to all your workers. A final point to consider is that employers in Tennessee might find that offering paid sick leave is necessary to attract and retain employees.

Non-Compete Agreements

Many employers ask employees to sign non-compete agreements when they are hired. The purpose of a non-compete is to protect proprietary information of the company and prevent the employee from setting up a competing business.

Non-compete agreements might make sense for senior managers who understand all the company's operations and processes or for employees with specialized knowledge. But these types of agreements rarely make sense with lower-level employees who lack knowledge about the company's overall operations and those who don't set corporate strategy.

In Tennessee, courts have become less inclined to enforce non-compete agreements unless the agreements are narrowly written. A non-compete that is limited to one or two years and to a small geographic area, such as one city or county, is more likely to be enforced than an agreement that is broadly written. Tennessee courts are also unlikely to enforce non-competes signed by lower-level employees.

On July 9, 2021, President Biden signed an executive order directing the Federal Trade Commission to review whether non-compete agreements are a restraint on business. The FTC was also instructed to review "unnecessary" occupational licenses that impede economic mobility.

Occupational licenses were originally created to ensure basic standards of competency and care for consumers. Unfortunately, licensing has become a barrier to entry with ever increasing educational requirements and rising license fees. States and local governments are happy to accommodate the License Raj because it generates millions of dollars in revenue each year. But the result is that licensing requirements are as effective a barrier to new entrants as a non-compete agreement.

> Before asking every employee to sign a non-compete agreement, ask yourself what exactly you are trying to protect. Locking in key employees with specialized skills or knowledge of your company's processes is important. But how much harm can the average employee truly do to your business?
>
> Employees should be free to move on, particularly if they aren't a good fit for your business. Rather than interfering with their ability to get another job, you might be able to protect your company's information and processes by asking the employee to sign a confidentiality agreement.
>
> A confidentiality agreement prohibits a former employee from sharing your company's secrets and proprietary information with third parties, including a new employer. It doesn't limit the former employee from working in your industry or for a competitor, as is usually the case with a non-compete agreement.

Joint Employer

Another hot issue facing employers relates to a National Labor Relations Board (NLRB) decision issued on August 27, 2015. In that decision, the NLRB changed the definition of "joint employer." Historically, an employer had to exercise control over the terms and conditions of employment in order to be deemed a joint employer. But the NLRB looked at whether a business has the potential to directly or indirectly control the terms of employment of another business's employees.

The new NLRB definition could have changed the relationship between a parent company and its subsidiary's employees or between a franchisor and a franchisee's employees. It could have also upset the relationship between a professional employer organization and the companies leasing employees from it.

The NLRB decision was appealed and spent several years meandering through administrative and court proceedings. Eventually, the case was remanded to the NLRB to clarify some of the details of its new definition of "joint employer." By then, a new president was in office and the voting members of the NLRB had changed. In 2020, the NLRB decided to withdraw the new "joint employer" definition. In 2021, a new presidential administration took another crack at the issue, although a final resolution is not yet available.

In August 2022, the NLRB proposed a new definition for joint employer that hinges on the "essential terms and conditions of employment." This phrase covers factors such as (a) wages, benefits, and other compensation; (b) hours of work and scheduling; (c) hiring and discharge; (d) discipline; (e) workplace health and safety; (f) supervision; (g) assignment; and (h) work rules and directions governing how the work is performed. Basically, the more control and supervision exercised by a parent company, the more likely there is a joint employer relationship.

Meanwhile, Tennessee didn't wait for the final outcome of the lawsuit against the NLRB. In March 2015, Tennessee amended the definition of "employee" in TCA §50-1-2 to say that a franchisor is not the employer of its franchisee's employees.

If your company operates a franchise model or leases employees through a professional employer organization (PEO), joint employment status might affect the relationship. Compare the 8 factors listed by the NLRB to your relationship with the franchisor or PEO. You might also ask an employment law attorney to explain the current definition of joint employment.

Terminating Employees

Terminating an unsatisfactory employee is a high-risk, low-reward responsibility for the employee's supervisor, the HR manager or the compliance officer and the company generally. So much can go wrong for so many reasons. An increasing risk is that an angry soon-to-be former employee will shoot up the workplace, killing their supervisor, the HR manager and co-workers whom the ex-employee blames for their termination. The non-violent former employees often allege wrongful termination based on a violation of the company's HR policies or anti-discrimination laws or retaliation. Retaliation is the most common claim investigated by the EEOC.

Retaliation is the most common claim investigated by the EEOC. An employer can be held liable for retaliating against an employee who filed an EEOC complaint, even when the employer never actually violated the law on which the complaint is based.

Wrongful termination claims commonly arise in the following situations. A former employee thinks a supervisor applied company rules unfairly, such as playing favorites. A former employee claims that the company failed to follow its own rules, such as the progressive discipline policy. Wrongful termination claims are more likely to be successful when the company fails to document the reasons justifying the decision to fire the employee.

Wrongful termination can arise when the company and the employee disagree about the date the employee was supposed to return from authorized leave. Imagine that an employee expects to return on Monday next week, but the company believes the leave ended on Monday of this week. The company treats the employee's failure to show up this Monday as a voluntary resignation; the employee argues that she or he was wrongfully terminated because the company got the date wrong.

Some of the most difficult wrongful termination claims arise in connection with employees who file workers compensation claims. Employees who are fired after they file a workers compensation claim or after they return from a leave of absence related to such a claim are likely to file suit alleging retaliation or discrimination (based on a disability acquired due to the injury). The threat of a wrongful termination claim can be reduced by having written policies and following those policies consistently in all situations.

Consider creating a disciplinary review committee to review termination requests by individual managers. The committee should consist of a senior business executive, an HR department representative, and a compliance person (if possible, the in-house attorney who advises the HR department).

This committee can ensure that company policies and applicable laws are followed to limit the chances of a terminated employee successfully alleging wrongful termination.

Create checklists to use during the hiring and firing processes, as they are a great way to keep the company representative (HR person or employee's manager) on track.

Separation of Employment form

In Tennessee, employers must notify the Tennessee Department of Labor and Workforce Development (Workforce) when an employee's status changes. This notice can be done by logging into your company's employer account at https://jobs4tn.gov. The employer can complete an on-line version of the Claimant Separation form, stating the reasons the employee was terminated.

This information will be critical if your company intends to dispute a claim for unemployment compensation filed by the former employee. A worker who voluntarily quits her or his job is not eligible for unemployment benefits. If the worker quit or was fired for cause, your company might want to challenge the former employee's claim for unemployment. That doesn't mean that your company will win its challenge, of course, but you'll want to preserve your right to dispute the claim.

Second, if your company has more than five employees, you are required to have a workers compensation policy for your employees. Your company will want the Department to know that the employee is no longer on your workers compensation policy. You will also need to notify your workers compensation insurer to take the employee off your policy.

Third, employers are now required to file quarterly payroll taxes with the Tennessee Department of Labor. Your payroll tax report shows who was employed in the preceding quarter. If your company completes the Claimant Separation form, it could save time responding to Department inquiries about why a particular employee is suddenly no longer appearing in your payroll tax report. The Department can look at your company's employer account to see that an employee is no longer working for your company.

Fourth and perhaps most importantly is that the termination information is helpful for both the employer and the former employee. Tennessee now has one database that shares information about government benefits. We've already looked at the unemployment claim situation. Here are a couple of other situations.

The termination information is shared with the Department of Human Services which reviews eligibility for TennCare (Medicaid). An unemployed worker or members of the former employee's household might be eligible for TennCare because the family's income dropped due to unemployment. The termination information is also entered into the child support database maintained by the Department of Children's Services (DCS). An unemployed worker is not going to be able to keep up with child support payments and DCS needs to know that.

The moral of the story is that your company can simplify its life by keeping the Tennessee government up to date on who is actually working for your company.

EMPLOYEE BENEFIT PROGRAMS

When we talk about employee benefits, most people think of the group health plan and retirement benefits. But employee benefits encompass more than these two important benefits.

Employee benefits include expenses such as reimbursement of business travel expenses, the cost of company-owned cell phones, tuition reimbursement and much more. These benefits are known as fringe benefits and are generally taxable income to employees. The IRS conveniently publishes an annual update on taxable fringe benefits in IRS Publication 15-B – Employer's Tax Guide to Fringe Benefits.

> Business owners should read IRS Publication 15-B – Employer's Tax Guide to Fringe Benefits, to get a general understanding of how the IRS taxes employee benefits. Of course, IRS publications are never fun to read so after you read the guide and become thoroughly frustrated at their "plain English," ask your CPA for assistance with questions you have about specific benefits.

Leave Policies

Employee benefits also include paid (and unpaid) leave, such as vacation and sick leave and paid time off. Paid leave is an employee benefit that is generally taxable income to the employee.

Taxing paid sick leave is a bit trickier because it depends on whether the employer or a third party pays the employee's sick leave. "Third party" refers to insurers who cover wage reimbursement when an employee is too sick to work, such as workers comp insurers or private insurers who offer short-term disability and long-term disability insurance to employees. The most widely recognized insurer is AFLAC. IRS Publication 15-A – Employer's Supplemental Tax Guide contains details on how employers should handle the taxes for paid sick leave. Read the Guide, then ask your CPA for help.

Leave policies generally fall within the scope of ERISA. ERISA is a complicated law dating back to 1974 and we can only skim the surface here. If you have in-depth questions related to ERISA, you will need to hire an attorney who specializes in ERISA issues. ERISA attorneys generally divide into sub-specialties depending on whether they focus on retirement plans, such as pension plans or 401(k) plans, or on employee welfare benefit plans, meaning the group health plan and related fringe benefits for employees.

ERISA

The key law when talking about employee benefits is the Employee Retirement Income Security Act of 1974 (ERISA). As its name implies, this law originated to protect pension benefits but it later evolved to include "employee welfare benefit" plans, meaning employer-sponsored group health plans and employee benefits related to the group health plan.

The law was passed in 1974 after Congressional hearings revealed widespread abuses of employee pensions by corporations. For example, corporations deducted money from an employee's paycheck that should have been deposited into the employee's pension account. Instead, the deducted funds often ended up in the corporation's general ledger account and were never deposited into the pension fund. As more workers retired, it became increasingly obvious that most pension funds were severely underfunded.

> An early series in the Doonesbury cartoon chronicled the adventures of Duke as he and some (possibly) organized crime buddies looted a pension fund. Duke later testified to the Congressional committee investigating pension fund fraud that he took the money because "the pension fund was just sitting there."

ERISA applies to all employers with a minimum of two employees. Churches and governmental entities, such as state governments or local governments, are generally exempt from ERISA. (There is an exception related to some of the group health plan requirements under the Affordable Care Act.) It sets deadlines for employers to deposit payroll deductions into pension accounts, including 401(k) plans. The law creates fiduciary responsibilities for employers and investment advisors that are intended to protect the funds due to employees.

ERISA sets standards for eligibility and participation in the group health plan and the pension or retirement plan. ERISA prohibits a company from setting up employee benefit programs that favor higher paid employees over the lower paid employees (the rank and file workers). ERISA also requires that similarly situated employees be treated the same.

ERISA incorporates a number of other federal laws that apply to group health plans, including COBRA, HIPAA privacy and non-discrimination rules and the use of genetic information by the group health plan.

Form 5500

ERISA requires an employer or the union representing workers or the health insurance company (depending on the type of benefit program) to file a Form 5500 with the U.S. Department of Labor (DOL) every year. As a general rule, a Form 5500 is required from each employer that (1) is subject to ERISA, (2) sponsors a group health plan or an employee retirement plan, including a 401(k) plan, and (3) has 100 or more employees.

The Form 5500 is a summary of the assets and liabilities of the pension plan or 401(k) plan and of the group health plan. Employers who lack the staff or expertise to prepare these annual filings might be able to outsource this reporting requirement to one of the consulting companies that specialize in preparing these filings. For example, some CPA firms and insurance brokers provide Form 5500 services. However, the employer remains responsible for the content of the Form 5500 and ensuring it is timely filed with the DOL.

Group Health Plans

Back in the 1930's Great Depression, the federal government worried about labor unrest in an age of mass unemployment and wage disputes. Congress debated how to reduce labor-management disputes without raising wages. The agreed solution was to improve employee benefit programs by encouraging employers to offer a group health plan to employees.

Employers receive a tax deduction for their contributions to the health plan's premiums which they can use to offset profits, thereby reducing the company's business taxes. The employee's portion of the health insurance premium is taken out of their wages before taxes, thereby reducing their personal taxable income.

An employee who receives health insurance through an employer is totally clueless about the true cost of health insurance in America. Most employees first learn of the true cost if they leave their jobs and become eligible for COBRA coverage, under which the employee must pay the full premium plus a two percent markup as an administrative fee.

Let's look at a simplistic model of health care costs: premium, deductible, co-pays and co-insurance.

Premium: This is the amount of money that an individual or a business must pay for the health insurance policy. When an employer offers a group health plan to employees, the employer and the employee split the premium with each paying a portion of the amount.

Deductible: This is the amount that the policy holder must pay for services and benefits covered by the insurance policy before the insurance company begins paying. In a group health plan, the employee is responsible for paying the deductible. Employers might help by contributing to a health savings account (HSA) or a flexible spending account (FSA).

Co-payment (co-pay): This is a dollar amount that the policy holder must pay for a specific service that is included in the health insurance policy. For example, many people must pay a co-pay for a doctor's visit or for a prescription. In a group health plan, the employee is responsible for paying the co-pay but the employer can help by contributing to an HSA or FSA.

Co-insurance: This is an amount that the policy holder and the insurance company split with each covering a portion of the charges owed on a service or benefit. For example, a particular type of surgery might have an 80/20 split, meaning the insurance company will pay 80% of the cost of the operation and the employee must pay the other 20%. In a group health plan, the employee is responsible for paying the co-pay but the employer can help by contributing to an HSA or FSA.

Out-of-Pocket: Your out-of-pocket costs include the deductible, co-pays, and co-insurance. This is the amount you will pay each policy year for your prescriptions and treatment by a doctor or hospital. There is a maximum annual limit for these charges. This amount is in addition to the premium you owe.

Health savings accounts and flexible spending accounts are creatures of the federal tax code. These accounts allow individuals to save money for medical expenses while also reducing the amount of taxes they owe on their wages. They are too complicated to be discussed in detail here. If your company has questions, talk to your health insurance agent (a/k/a benefits producer).

Types of Group Health Plans

Historically, an employer bought a group health plan and divided the cost of the premium with employees. An employee's cost also included deductibles, co-payments, and co-insurance for the services provided under the insurance coverage. The structure of group health plans come in several formats.

A. "Traditional" group health plan

A "traditional" group health plan usually involves a health maintenance organization (HMO) or a preferred provider organization (PPO). The employer and employee share the cost of the premium with the employee's portion deducted from payroll. In addition, the employee will also owe co-pays, deductibles and co-insurance for the health services used. Under this format, the employer gets a tax deduction for its part of the premium and the employee's portion is deducted from her/ his paycheck "pre-tax" meaning before payroll taxes are assessed, which lowers the employee's taxable income. Under these plans, the insurance company is usually responsible for filing the Form 5500.

B. High Deductible Health Plan (HDHP)

Under an HDHP, the premium is lower because most of the health care costs are shifted to the employee. The employer and employee each pay a portion of the premium. But the employee pays for all health care costs until the deductible is reached, after which the employee pays a co-pay or co-insurance just like a "traditional" health care plan. The deductible can range from $1000 to $5000 or even higher. To help the employee cover the deductible, an HDHP must always offer the employee a health savings account (HSA). The employee's contributions to an HSA are made on a pre-tax basis, which lowers the employee's taxable wages. This means that both employer and employee get a tax break on funding the health plan and the HSA. Under these plans, the insurance company is usually responsible for filing the Form 5500.

C. Cafeteria plan

These plans are also called "Section 125" plans after the federal tax code section that authorized them. Under these plans, an employee is offered a variety of benefits including at least one taxable benefit (usually cash) and "qualified benefits" paid on a pre-tax basis. "Qualified benefits" include health care, dental and vision care, dependent care assistance, and a flexible spending account (FSA). Since "qualified benefits" are not considered wages under federal tax law, an employee's contributions to an FSA are made pre-tax, reducing the employee's taxable wages. Under these plans, the employer must file the Form 5500 with the U.S. Department of Labor.

Each of these types of health plans still exist under the Affordable Care Act (ACA). The major change is that ACA-compliant health plans must offer minimum essential coverage, which is defined below.

Affordable Care Act ("Obamacare")

In 2010, the Affordable Care Act (ACA or Obamacare) was enacted amid much controversy. Since 2010, some politicians have repeatedly promised to overturn the law but failed after being unable to agree on the details of a plan to replace the requirements of the ACA. Surveys now show that most Americans prefer to keep the ACA with limited amendments to expand coverage, particularly premium assistance for the working poor.

Two of the key reasons Americans have come to love the ACA are that the law prohibits pre-existing condition exclusions, and it reduces the waiting period for coverage. Individuals with chronic conditions such as hypertension, heart disease and diabetes, historically found that these conditions were excluded from coverage. Another annoyance was that individuals often faced lengthy waiting periods lasting from 90 days to 120 days before the coverage finally became effective.

Another popular feature of the ACA is that adult children up to age 26 can remain on a parent's health plan rather than "aging out" at the age of 18. Many parents appreciate the convenience of keeping their college kids as dependents on their employer's group health plan.

The ACA changed how the entire healthcare insurance industry works, from hospitals to insurance companies to prescription drug coverage; from individual health policies to employer-provided group health plans. One important change was to extend ERISA requirements of eligibility and participation to all group health plans. Previously, only self-insured plans were required to comply with ERISA.

Prior to the ACA, many companies offered generous health coverage with no out-of-pocket costs and few coverage limitations to senior management and their dependents. At the same time, lower-level employees were offered health plans with substantial out-of-pocket costs and limited coverage, including no coverage for pre-existing conditions.

Since the ACA was enacted, ERISA rules require employers to treat similarly situated employees the same for purposes of eligibility and participation in the group health plan. ERISA also establishes seven bona fide employment categories of similarly situated employees. They are (1) full-time versus part-time status, (2) different geographic location, (3) membership in a collective bargaining unit, (4) date of hire, (5) length of service, (6) current employee versus former employee status, and (7) different occupations. Employees within each category must be offered the same coverage and opportunity to enroll in the coverage.

To understand the ACA, it helps to know some of the key terms used in the ACA.

Key Terms in ACA

A group health plan offered by an employer must have premium and coverage categories that fit within each of these key terms.

Minimum essential coverage (MEC): This term refers to the types of services that must be included in an ACA-compliant health policy. There are ten categories: ambulatory patient services; emergency services; maternity and newborn care; pediatric (children's) services including dental and vision care; rehabilitative/habilitative services and devices; mental health and substance use disorder services including behavioral health treatment; preventive and wellness services and chronic disease management; prescription drug coverage; laboratory services; and hospitalization. These categories are also known as essential health benefits (EHB).

Affordability: This term applies to the employee's portion of the premium for employee-only health coverage. The employer and the employee each contribute a portion of the premium charged. The ACA limits the percentage of wages that can be used to pay the employee's portion of employee-only coverage. This affordability rule does not apply to the premium charged for family coverage. In 2010, the employee's premium payment was deemed affordable if it did not exceed 9.5% of the employee's W-2 wages. This percentage is adjusted each year. For example, in 2022, the rate for the employee-only premium was 9.61% of an employee's W-2 wages.

Actuarial value of benefits: This term refers to the employee's portion of the cost of the health services covered by the policy, which the employee pays via deductibles, co-pays, and co-insurance. The insurance company and the employee share the costs of the health services on one of the following bases: 90/10, 80/20, 70/30, or 60/40.

Most employers offer a group health plan that is a bronze level plan with a 60/40 actuarial value. A bronze level plan meets the ACA minimum requirements. Under these plans, the individual must cover 40% of the costs for the health services used. Many employers also offer an 80/20 (gold level plan) for employees who want to pay a higher premium in exchange for lower out-of-pocket costs for the health services used.

Large and Small Employers

The ACA divides employers into two categories: large employers and small employers. A small employer has fewer than 50 employees. A large employer has 50 or more employees.

Deciding who is a small or a large employer is not as simple as just counting the number of names on the payroll sheet. Under the ACA, employers must count full-time and part-time workers. For employers in industries like hospitality and construction, where work schedules might vary each week, the ACA includes two formulas for assessing whether these "variable hour" employees are eligible for coverage.

To be eligible for an offer of health insurance coverage, an employee must work an average of 30 hours per week during the counting period set by the employer. Most employers use the Lookback Method, in which they review hours worked by each employee during the previous 12-month period.

Don't drive yourself insane trying to understand the Lookback Method of calculating an employee's eligibility for the group health plan. Most payroll software now includes algorithms to do the calculations automatically. If your payroll software doesn't, consider an upgrade to a new payroll platform. If all else fails, ask your insurance agent (a/k/a, benefits producer) for help.

The ACA sets the *minimum* requirements for employers who offer health insurance coverage to their employees. Employers can always offer more than these minimums if it is financially feasible or necessary to attract and retain employees. Some examples of employers offering more include:

- Paying the full premium for employee-only coverage.
- Offering health coverage to part-time employees.
- Contributing money to a health savings account or flexible spending account to help cover the employee's out-of-pocket costs.

Employer Penalty

The ACA originally included a requirement that every individual obtain health coverage, either through an individual policy or through an employer's group health plan. To nudge people into obtaining health coverage, the ACA included an individual penalty which was assessed against any tax refund owed to the individual. The ACA also nudged "large" employers to offer a group health plan by imposing an employer penalty.

In 2017, the individual penalty for not having ACA-compliant health insurance was reduced to zero. This meant that individuals were still liable for not having health insurance, but the dollar amount of the penalty was zero. Everyone's tax refund was safe again, at least for ACA purposes.

The employer penalty is more complicated because it arises from two separate obligations of the employer. The first obligation is set out at 26 USC §4980H which said that large employers were subject to a penalty if they failed to offer an affordable health plan (meaning a bronze plan) to eligible employees. The penalty for failing to offer an affordable health plan was eventually reduced to zero.

That's where the second obligation for large employers complicated life. The IRS required employers to prove they had offered affordable coverage by filing IRS Form 1095. A Form 1095 was completed for each W-2 employee showing the (1) employee was eligible for an offer of health insurance, (2) employee was offered coverage in the employer's group health plan, and (3) employee-only premium was affordable.

In IRS lingo, Form 1095 is an "informational" return. Failure to file this form means the IRS can assess a penalty. When the IRS assesses a penalty, it guestimates the amount owed based on the penalties allowed under §4980H multiplied by the number of employees. By the time employers receive a demand letter from the IRS, the penalty may be large enough to threaten the financial future of the company.

This meant that employers could not be assessed a penalty for failing to offer affordable coverage. But they could be assessed a penalty for failing to file Form 1095 proving they had offered affordable coverage. If all that seems confusing, it is!

What Has Not Changed

Some responsibilities have not been changed. For example, employers must notify employees about the healthcare Marketplace. The Marketplace is an internet portal. The portal might be run by the state government or by the U.S. Department of Health & Human Services (HHS). The Marketplace website allows individuals to compare individual health policies available in their geographical area based on the premium and out-of-pocket costs. The policies are divided into categories as bronze, silver, gold, or platinum policies. A bronze plan has the lowest premium but the highest out-of-pocket costs for the insured.

Lower income individuals may be eligible for financial assistance to pay the premium on their health plan. This assistance is called a premium subsidy. Eligibility is based on the individual's entire household income in comparison to the federal poverty level.

Employees who are not offered health coverage by their employers may also buy individual coverage via the Marketplace. Alternatively, some employees may waive their employer's group health plan and buy individual health coverage via the Marketplace. However, employees who waive their employers' coverage are usually not eligible for any of the premium subsidies available to lower income individuals who apply through the Marketplace.

> By this point, your head is probably ready to explode. How can a small business owner or an HR manager or a compliance officer ever learn all the details lurking in the ACA?
>
> The answer is: don't even try.
>
> When your company is ready to offer a group health plan, find an experienced benefits producer, meaning an insurance agent licensed to sell group health plans to employers, who can assist you in the process. The benefits producer can search for coverage that best matches what you would like to do for your employees with what your budget will allow.

Medicare v. the Group Health Plan

Employees who are 65 years old are usually eligible for both their employer's group health plan and for Medicare. These employees must decide whether to enroll in their employer's plan or in Medicare. To avoid unnecessary heartache for employees and their employers, there are a few general rules to keep in mind.

The general rule is that an employer is prohibited from nudging or pushing older employees out of the group health plan and into enrolling for Medicare coverage. This ploy was tried by large companies that could afford to pay the penalties assessed by the Centers for Medicare and Medicaid Services (CMS), a subsidiary of the U.S. Department of Health and Human Services.

Unless your small company has buckets of extra cash, it's best to learn from the mistakes of your larger competitors. Of course, the general rule comes with two huge caveats.

The first caveat is that when an employer has <u>fewer than 20 employees</u>, Medicare is the <u>primary</u> health insurance for older workers. That means any Medicare-eligible older employee <u>must</u> enroll in Medicare to have primary health coverage. If they don't, they will effectively have no health insurance because the employer's group health plan is secondary coverage and will only cover claims not paid by Medicare.

The second caveat reverses this order. If an employer has <u>more than 20 employees</u>, then Medicare is <u>secondary</u> health insurance. That means any Medicare-eligible older workers should enroll in the employer's group health plan because the group health plan is the <u>primary</u> health insurance.

Please note that the Medicare rules related to employer group health plans are fiendishly complicated. If you are the owner, HR manager or compliance officer for your small company, talk to an experienced health insurance agent, a consultant who specializes in Medicare issues, or to a health law attorney who is familiar with these issues.

Retirement Plans

Workers today have a couple of options for financially supporting themselves in their older years after they retire. The option that most Americans rely on is the Social Security Administration's retirement benefit. This benefit was created in the 1930's to counteract labor unrest caused by the Great Depression.

During your working life, a portion of your payroll deductions are contributed to the Social Security retirement fund. After you retire (at full retirement age), you will receive a monthly check based on your lifetime earnings up to a maximum of about $3300 a month. But the average monthly benefit is only around $1600 a month, which is clearly insufficient to cover rent, utilities and food.

> In the 1880's, Prussia became the first country in the world to offer universal workers compensation, disability, health, and retirement benefits. Chancellor Otto von Bismarck didn't care about the workers as much as he worried about a worker revolution interrupting the industrial and military might of Prussia. He rammed through the reforms to outmaneuver his socialist and Marxist political opponents.

The inadequacy of the Social Security retirement benefit means that most of us need another source of retirement funds. That is why the second most common option for covering retirement is through an employer-sponsored retirement plan.

Pension Plans and 401(k) Plans

When ERISA was created, most companies offered "defined benefits" pension plans. Under these plans, the risk on the investments was covered by the employers. These plans paid a monthly amount based on the employee's final salary and guaranteed a specific dollar amount would be paid monthly until the employee died. To no one's eventual surprise, defined benefit pension plans proved an expensive failure.

Defined benefits pension plans were designed at a time when people did much more physically demanding work, often in manufacturing, which literally wore out their bodies. Many workers retired at age 65 and passed on to their just reward before they reached the age of 75.

But as retirees lived longer, healthier lives, defined pension plans ran out of money. In some cases, pension plans were underfunded when employers miscalculated (the kindest interpretation) the expected rate of return on investments in stocks and bonds that would be needed to cover the promises made to retirees. In some cases, employers simply diverted pension fund contributions to support other corporate activities. By 1974, pension fund insolvencies and the angry voters with no retirement funds caused Congress to act to clean up the mess by passing ERISA.

> The only defined benefits retirement plans that you are likely to find in the U.S. today are the plans for state govern- ment employees or municipal workers like fire fighters and police officers. Many states, counties and cities already pay higher interest rates on the bonds they issue because of the risks associated with their underfunded pension plans.
>
> The ugly secret that your state and local elected offi- cials don't want you to notice until long after they are out of office is that taxpayers are on the hook for these grossly underfunded plans. At some point, taxes must go up to fulfill the promises made to public employees or the government must default on its debt or both. Several cities and the terri- tory of Puerto Rico have already suffered this fate.

These days virtually all employers offer "defined contribution" plans. The most common is a 401(k) plan, named after the federal tax code sec- tion that created these types of plans. Under a 401(k) plan, the employee bears the risk that the rate of return on the stocks and bonds will be sufficient to pay for retirement. Employee contributions can be topped up by employers who usually offer to match an employee's contributions up to a specific dollar amount or a percentage of wages. The employ- er's contribution is only "earned" by the employee when the employee becomes fully vested in the plan, which usually happens after six years.

Employees who leave before they fully vest may take their contributions along when they leave. Usually, the employee will "roll over" the money into their new employer's 401(k) plan or into an individual retirement account (IRA).

The major risk involved with either type of retirement plan is a violation of the relevant fiduciary duties. A person who holds a fiduciary responsibility is obligated to protect the assets in the retirement plan and to make prudent business decisions about investing the plan assets.

The ERISA regulations for retirement plans are regularly tweaked by the Employee Benefits Security Administration (EBSA), a division of the U.S. Department of Labor. Each rule change is hotly debated by employers, investment companies, investment advisors and anyone who actually understands what the rule changes will do for retirees.

As the owner, or HR manager or compliance officer for your company, you probably do not have time to become an expert on these risks. So don't waste your time going down the rabbit hole of ERISA regulations. Ask for help from the administrator of your company's 401(k) plan or an attorney who specializes in ERISA retirement plan compliance.

Auto Enrollment in 401(k) P lans

For decades, the Department of Labor (DOL), employers, and investment advisors have encouraged employees to enroll in their company's 401(k) plan. The contributions are deducted before taxes are taken out of an employee's wages, which lowers the employee's taxable wages. Most employers offer to match the employee's contribution, whether as a specific dollar amount or a percentage of the employee's wages or salary. The employer match is akin to free money for employees.

Unfortunately, no incentive has been sufficient to convince many employees to voluntarily enroll in their company's 401(k) plan. Some lower wage employees worry that another deduction from their paycheck will mean they can't afford to pay their current monthly bills. But many employees are apparently unaware of the true cost of supporting themselves after they retire.

As a result, the EBSA has considered issuing regulations that require employers to automatically enroll eligible employees into the company's 401(k) plan. Employees would then need to sign an "opt out" form asking to be removed from the plan. The hope is that more employees will stay enrolled so that they have more than just their Social Security retirement checks in their probably not-at-all golden years.

INFORMATION
SYSTEMS

The information systems (IS) or information technology (IT) department is probably the fastest evolving department at your company. Technology has lowered the cost of starting a business. Any company can pay a subscription for cloud-based software programs and data storage rather than owning computer hardware and software. Internet connections with Wi-Fi mean you can work from anywhere. The internet also allows even the smallest business to sell its service or product anywhere.

Of course, all that freedom comes with two big risks: cybersecurity and privacy laws that protect your customers' and your employees' data. Here's a quick overview of these risks.

Cyber-security

The risks involved with a security breach of company records are difficult to quantify. Every year criminals steal billions of dollars of personal data, including credit card numbers, dates of birth, Social Security numbers, residential addresses or even personal health information. This personal information is sold by hackers on the dark web to other criminals who use the information for identity theft.

Some hackers specialize in seizing control of a business's databases with the goal of ransoming the information back to the business. Companies that can't afford the ransom or refuse to pay might be permanently locked out of their own databases. Meanwhile, the hackers will likely sell the information to others.

Another thriving area of criminal activity is industrial espionage, in which a company's patented or proprietary information is stolen. Industrial espionage is usually carried out by government agents who are seeking to give their domestic industries a quick boost in the marketplace. In recent years, China and Russia have been accused of using personnel from their respective military's cybersecurity units to hack into business and government databases. Russia increased its cyber-attacks after invading Ukraine in February 2022, trying to intimidate and blackmail the U.S. and its allies into dropping their support for Ukraine.

Cam started the Glamor Guide on a shoe-string budget and used free services, like Google Docs, for her business records. As the business grew, she upgraded the technology to keep up with her expanding workforce. But she continued using the same password for multiple programs because it was easier for her to remember. Besides, her company was so small, she doubted it would attract notice.

This morning when she arrived at work and cranked up her laptop, she shrieked in horror and hyperventilated until she passed out. Her assistant arrived to find Cam slumped at her desk with espresso puddling on the desk, out cold. She looked at the message scrolling across the laptop's screen. It said, "The weenies of wonderland strike again! You've been hacked, stupid."

Her assistant revived Cam and they called the police to report the crime. The police told them to call the FBI, which handles cybercrime claims.

Small businesses can make their data a less attractive target by following reasonable and prudent practices to protect their data. Companies are expected to keep their IT firewalls up to date to limit the opportunities for hackers to steal information. But IT firewalls have trouble staying ahead of hackers and, anyway, many breaches of security occur due to user error. For example, passwords aren't changed or are easy to guess or companies decide to save money on cybersecurity upgrades.

These days, most employees and independent contractors use their personal cell phones, iPads and laptops to access company databases. That's wonderful for employees who like working from home or at the nearest coffee shop. Workers can do their jobs or projects from anywhere which increases productivity while reducing company expenses to rent office space. But that can be bad because it also increases the points of entry for nefarious sorts. To limit this risk, many companies require employees to allow the company's IT department to remotely access a device and terminate access to company databases.

The frequency of cyber-attacks has increased significantly. The Cybersecurity and Infrastructure Security Agency (CISA), an agency under the Department of Homeland Security, coordinates cybersecurity efforts with other governmental entities and private organizations. One private organization is a non-profit, the National Cyber Security Alliance (https://staysafeonline.org/cybersecure-business/), which has a plethora of resources for protecting against and responding to cyber-attacks. The NCSA includes many how-to guides for small companies to help them identify cybersecurity gaps and take practical steps to reduce the risks.

Federal and state laws put the burden on companies to ensure their databases are secure from cyber threats, particularly databases containing customer information. If a company is hit with a cyberattack, the company must notify the appropriate federal and state regulatory authority about the data breach.

The type of information stolen affects which regulator must be notified of the security breach. For example, if hackers steal customer information or lock your database, your company's first step should be to report the crime to the local FBI office so that it can track the criminals in hopes of recovering the data or the ransom money. Your company will also need to comply with the consumer protection laws administered by the Federal Trade Commission (FTC) rules which require a company to notify its customers so that the customers can take steps to protect themselves from identity theft.

> Protect your company!
> - Don't share passwords.
> - Require passwords to be changed periodically, say, every 90 days.
> - Require 2-step authentication when signing into a database.
> - Conduct regular checks to ensure that all software has been updated with the latest patches released by the vendor that created the software.
> - Use a password protector service, like 1 Password, Dashlane, NordPass, or a similar app.

Privacy

Privacy issues come in two forms: a consumer's right to control digital content about them (the right to be forgotten) and database breaches. We've already looked at database breaches. Take a look at some recent laws covering control of digital content.

The General Data Protection Regulation (GDPR) became effective on May 28, 2018, in the European Union. But the GDPR reaches far beyond the geographical area of the European Union thanks to the internet. Anyone anywhere in the world can theoretically access your website. That means your company can't afford to ignore the GDPR because a person living in the European Union could access your company's website to buy your services or products, leaving their personal information behind as part of the transaction.

The purpose of the GDPR is to allow individuals more control over how their personal information is accessed and stored and shared in cyberspace. Individuals have the "right to be forgotten" by having their data removed from social media sites during their lifetimes or after the individual dies. Companies must notify individuals of what personal information they collect when an individual accesses a company's website. While the focus of the GDPR is on social media giants like Meta (formerly Facebook) and retailers like Amazon, the law is very broadly written to take in internet transactions of businesses of all sizes.

Another recent privacy law is the California Consumer Privacy Act (CCPA) which became effective on January 1, 2020. If your company has customers that live in California, those customers have the right to know what personal information your company collects on them and how you use that information. The CCPA also requires full disclosure of financial charges in credit transactions for for-profit companies. If you're selling services or products to California-based consumers, you might need to provide additional details of the charges. Another feature of the CCPA is that it restricts garnishments, which will affect debt collection companies.

Don't try to figure out these privacy laws on your own. Check the resources on the Federal Trade Commission's (FTC) website and talk to an experienced IT vendor that provides network security for small businesses.

Hardware and Software

It is easier than ever to start a new business because the technology hurdles have disappeared. Laptops and iPads are cheap compared to desktop computers and their servers.

Expensive telephone networks are no longer necessary either. Most small businesses operate via cellphones or a cloud-based telephone service. Video conferencing is also much easier and cheaper with applications like Google Meet, Microsoft Teams, and Zoom, to name the best known.

Software options range from free services, such as GoogleDocs, to subscription services, like Microsoft's Office 365 suite of applications. Along with cloud-based applications like GoogleDocs and Office 365, small businesses can buy storage space online from a plethora of companies, such as Dropbox, Microsoft, Amazon Web Services (AWS). Some IT vendors for small businesses offer internet-based data storage, often leasing storage space from Microsoft or AWS.

These days, many small companies have employees or independent contractors spread across several time zones, with some located outside the U.S. To ensure projects stay on track, there are many project management software options, including Asana, ClickUp, Basecamp, Monday and Trello. Some of these software options are designed for specific industries.

> Start with the free services. As your company grows, find a local IT vendor that can set up an intranet for your company's data. These IT vendors usually provide an outsourced "help desk" to troubleshoot your IT problems. Most now also offer cybersecurity services and cloud-based storage when you need an upgrade from Dropbox.

Of course, this wonderful, mostly low-cost world comes with a new set of hassles because people are involved. As your company grows, so do the HR headaches. For example, when employees use their personal electronic devices, such as their cellphones, laptops and iPads, for business, it becomes harder to draw a line between working and not working. Some employees may be owed overtime pay if they continue working outside their normally scheduled hours.

Think of it. An hourly worker responds to emails every evening causing her to routinely work a 50-hour workweek. Since she's an hourly (non-exempt) employee, she's owed overtime pay for each hour in excess of 40 hours during that workweek. To avoid having this type of scenario bite your bottom line, your company needs to clearly set expectations for employees about when they need to stop working.

The other headache for business is that an employee's personal devices might become new entry points for cyberthieves. So if you allow your employees to use their personal devices for business, you will need a policy that requires them to routinely update their on-line security. Your business will also need a way to remotely terminate access to your business's databases and systems if the device is stolen, or lost, or the employee is fired.

Bottom line: As your company grows, pay for tech support. One of the best decisions you'll ever make as a small business owner is the decision to pay for tech support. A small business will need a data management system to store company records, including information about customers. Your small business will also need a way to protect proprietary and confidential information.

Records Retention

The IT department is often responsible for records retention, since it maintains the databases containing company records. Records retention involves asking: what is a "business record" and how long does a company need to hang on to the information before destroying it? The answer varies depending on the type of business records involved. For example, most companies hang on to tax information for seven to ten years because, depending on the type of claim, the applicable statute of limitations for IRS claims is ten years.

Of course, not all records need to be held for ten years. When deciding how long to keep business records, an owner, HR manager or compliance officer can look at the applicable statute of limitations. For example, the general federal statute of limitations is 6 years for contracts claims and 3 years for tort (personal injury) claims. In Tennessee there are many limitations periods, although most will range from one year to six years.

It is important to review both federal and state laws when setting your company's records retention policy. Ask an attorney for assistance, if necessary. After all, the attorney will be relying on your company's records, or the lack of them, to defend your business if you are sued.

Below are some suggested retention period for different types of documents. These retention periods correspond to the statute of limitations that apply to claims or lawsuits involving those types of documents. This is not a complete list of all the statutes of limitations under federal or

Tennessee state laws that might apply to your company. It covers only the most common types of documents.

Suggested Retention Period	Type of record
Permanent	Company records (e.g., Charter, Articles of Incorporation, Operating Agreement). Property records, trust deeds.
7 – 10 years	Bank records.
7 years	Software and hardware inventory details.
6 years	Tax records – company, from the last accounting period.
5 years	Tax records - self-employed or partnership, from the last tax date. Employee personnel files, from date of termination of employment.
3 years	Form I-9, from date of termination of employment. Sickness/sick pay records, from date of termination of employment.
6 months	Resumes, job applications of those not hired. Email correspondence. But emails with critical information (e.g., contract negotiation details or information about decisions that legally bind the company), should follow the retention period applicable to that type of information.

To Shred or Not to Shred – That is the Question

An effective record retention policy will require your business to regularly get rid of documentation when the retention period expires.

Physical copies must be shredded and electronic copies must be deleted. That means someone at your company must create a calendar to ensure that company records are properly destroyed at the right time. Most companies shred old records with the assistance of a vendor that provides data management services. There are many vendors, from national companies like Iron Mountain to locally based companies. Always get a couple of quotes before signing on the dotted line.

When choosing an archiving vendor for your company's data, ask the following:

- How easy is it to search their archiving system that holds your company's data?
- Do they offer both physical and electronic storage options?
- What are their monthly fees to store, meaning to archive, your company's data?
- Does this fee include the cost of shredding or disposing of your data when the records retention policy says the records should be destroyed?
- What add-on fees do they charge (e.g., do you pay an extra fee if you need to retrieve some stored information)?

Why is shredding on a schedule so critical? Expect your business to be sued or to be threatened with a lawsuit. That's America. If your business is sued by an angry customer or vendor or employee, the company will need to produce reams of corporate documents to the opposing side during the pre-trial discovery phase. Discovery requests are usually worded to capture the maximum amount of information in your company's corporate records. If you've properly followed the record retention policy, you might have already disposed of older information as part of your routine records retention policy.

Of course, there is a season for not shredding too. If your company is already in a lawsuit, the judge will expect your company to suspend its usual shredding schedule. Even if your company has not yet been sued, if you reasonably believe that your company is about to be sued, you must stop shredding. Lawyers call this "in anticipation of litigation". If you continue shredding documents, a judge may assess monetary fines or (much worse) deny some of your legal defenses. Not to mention that your company will make the evening news for all the wrong reasons.

COMPANY-WIDE RISKS

Each area of the company has unique risks which contribute to company-wide risks. In our final section of this book, we will look at company-wide risks that need to be addressed in an effective corporate compliance program.

Succession Planning

One of the most common risks faced by a company is failure to plan for the future. This issue is becoming acute as Baby Boomers retire or die and their businesses are passed to the next generation. Many companies fail when the founder dies or retires. Aside from the founder, there are workers who must be replaced as they are promoted or retire. A succession plan enhances the chances of a smooth transition and the continued good financial health of the company.

It's not easy to talk about this subject because if you're the founder, you may be reluctant to retire because you think that no one can adequately replace you. No one likes to contemplate their own death either. But as a business owner, you have a fiduciary responsibility to do what is best for the business. The task of the company's compliance officer is to explain to senior management the risks of a failure to plan. It is then up to senior management to make a business decision to mitigate the risk.

> Cam started The Glamor Guide in hopes that she would leave a successful company as a legacy for her children. They have all worked in the business, moving into different roles over time so that they would learn how to run the business. But instead of paying attention to the details that Cam wants them to learn, they seem fixated on re-enacting every child-hood rivalry.
>
> Lately, Cam has worried that her bickering children have turned her glam business into a knockoff version of *The Godfather* or *Succession*. In desperation, she has decided to create a succession plan in hopes of saving the future of her company from her bratty kids, even if that means appointing someone outside the family to run it.

The other reason to plan for the future is to grow smoothly. Whatever your rank in the corporate hierarchy, it helps to remember that your path to promotion depends on training a replacement for your current job. To train your replacement you will need to clearly define the process for performing the tasks assigned to your job description. Written processes are basically training tools to ensure the same company functions are done the same way every time, thus ensuring quality of the work performed.

Disaster Planning and Recovery

Every company must be prepared to continue functioning during a crisis or disaster, and then to recover from the disaster. A disaster can be caused by natural acts, such as a tornado or flood, or it can be man-made (unnatural?) such as power outages and stock market crashes that freeze credit availability.

Many small businesses skimp on this risk because the owners are busy with daily operations. They seldom take the time to think strategically about big picture items, like how to survive a disaster.

In 2010, Nashville, Tennessee was inundated with 13 inches of rain in less than three days. The Great Flood of 2010 left homes and businesses literally and financially under water. Companies with disaster plans and business continuity plans were able to locate their employees to confirm they were safe and to keep their employees updated about the company. These businesses were also able to reopen their doors quickly because they had a plan for their recovery. Business as usual was infinitely easier for individuals and companies that had planned in advance how they would handle a disaster.

A disaster plan (DP) is a step-by-step guide on dealing with a disaster as it happens. A business continuity plan (BCP) is the framework for returning to normalcy after the crisis ends. These plans can be separated into two documents or combined into one comprehensive document. When creating your DP and BCP consider the following questions:

1. Building:
   a. What will we do if we can't use our office space?
   b. Can employees work from home or do we need alternate office space?
   c. How will our customers and suppliers/vendors find us?

2. People:
   a. How will we communicate with our employees during a crisis?
   b. How will the company continue normal business activities if most of the employees are unavailable as a result of the disaster?
   c. How do we inform our customers and vendors about our situation?

3. Technology:
   a. What will we do if we lose our phones, computer systems, etc.?
   b. How will we replace the technology?
   c. What will we do if we can't access electronic company records?
   d. How will we recreate lost business records, whether paper files or electronic files?

These questions should naturally lead you to many more questions about the details of how your company operates and how it will survive a disaster. As you begin gathering information, you might have questions about how to organize the information into a usable plan. Using a template will help you stay organized.

There are many DP and BCP templates readily available from trade organizations or websites that you can adapt to your company's specific situation. Using a template will also ensure that you don't forget any key functions that need to be covered in the plan.

After you create a DP and a BCP, it needs to be tested. Testing your disaster plan is a bit like the military playing war games. The military creates an imaginary crisis and then sets their plan in motion. As they react to the crisis, they are looking for points of failure where the plan doesn't work. Then they adapt their plan so that in a future similar crisis, the plan works more effectively.

Testing your disaster plan is a bit like a military war game without olive-drab uniforms and cool toys. Your enemy will be fires, floods, tornadoes, or active shooter situations that interrupt business as usual.

The goal is the same – to look for points of failure where the plan doesn't work. Then you can fix your plan to work properly before a disaster hits.

Of course, things will still become screwed up in an actual emergency, but that's to be expected. As the military adage goes, "no plan survives first contact with the enemy." But having a plan that you have tested will allow you to improvise during the crisis so that you are better able to protect your company and your employees.

Risk management experts recommend regularly testing your disaster recovery plan. Many companies conduct drills at least once a year to test their plans. Practice might not make perfect, but it will reduce the likelihood of a panicked and incoherent reaction when the crisis hits. You will also be testing your business continuity plan to see how easily your company can return to business as usual. Routinely testing your company's DP and BCP will do two things for your company. First, it will guarantee that someone remembers where the written plan was stashed after the last drill. Second, you will be able to identify new points of failure that need to be fixed.

Corporate Insurance Programs

The most common method for addressing corporate-wide risk is through insurance. Business insurance programs can be divided into two broad categories: required insurance and prudent insurance.

Examples of required insurance are: worker's compensation insurance, which is mandatory for any Tennessee employer with five or more employees; liability insurance that a landlord requires of a tenant; and commercial auto coverage for company-owned vehicles, such as company cars or delivery trucks.

Examples of prudent coverage are: directors' and officers' liability policies to cover these individuals for alleged wrongdoing while performing their duties; employment practices liability policies which cover a variety of claims against the company and individual managers, such as employee allegations of sexual harassment or discrimination; and property coverage, including business interruption coverage and coverage for replacement of computers and other technology.

Although none of the insurance policies in the second category are required by law or contract, they can make the difference to the financial survival of a company in the event of a disaster. Of course, few companies can afford to buy all of the prudent coverage that is available. So do a Tennessee two-step: (1) identify your key risks and (2) buy coverage that will reduce the threat that those risks can put you out of business.

Assessing the risks is generally the responsibility of the compliance officer. For many small businesses, that means the company owner is responsible for assessing the risks. Ultimately, the company's owner or senior management team must decide how to mitigate the risks. Risks are mitigated by (1) selecting the insurance policy or policies that cover the biggest risks currently faced by the company and (2) adjusting the coverage later as the risks change or as your budget increases. Remember that your insurance agent or broker can be a great resource in helping you select the coverage that best fits your current risks and budget.

A Quick Review of the Insurance Industry

When you first talk to your company's insurance agent or broker, you might hear industry-specific terms that are new to you. Here are some key terms and phrases.

Insurance involves a triangular relationship:

Insured: The individual or corporate entity that pays the premiums owed and is covered by the insurance policy that is purchased.

Agent: The person who sells the insurance coverage to the insured. In Tennessee, this person might be called a "producer" or a "broker." Each agent must be licensed by the state insurance department. The agent must also be appointed by each insurer that authorizes the agent to sell the insurer's products. The agent usually works for an agency (a/k/a, broker or brokerage), which is a business entity that is licensed by the state insurance department and appointed by each insurer.

Insurer: The insurance company that creates the insurance policy that you are buying and pays any claims against the policy. The insurer is also known as the "carrier" or the "underwriter." The insurer's policy details and premium rates must be filed with and approved by the state insurance department in the state where the policy will be sold.

The insured buys a "policy" which will have the following parts:

1.   Declarations page - A snapshot of the coverage, the policy term (when it begins and when it ends), and the premium paid. Your agent/broker will probably call it the "dec" page. There is a section listing the form numbers for all endorsements or riders that are incorporated into the policy

2.   Terms and Conditions - This is the basic insurance contract and it will consist of many pages of small print. Many people refer to this part of the policy as the "boilerplate" because it is standardized information. A key section is the Claims notice section which tells you when and how to file a claim. The policy will have one of the following bases for making a claim:

3.   Claims made policy: These policies have a defined retroactive date and an extended reporting period, which applies if the policy is cancelled. The loss must be incurred after the defined retroactive date and the claim must be reported to or filed with the insurer during the policy period including the extended reporting period. This is the most common type of claims language in a policy.

4.   Occurrence based policy: The loss must take place during the policy period regardless of when the claim is made to the insurer. This type of claims language in a policy is rare.

5.   Exclusions - This section of the Terms and Conditions tells you what is not covered in your policy.

6.   Endorsements or Riders - These pages are additions to the underlying policy that modify the underlying Terms and Conditions of the policy. Each endorsement or rider has a form number. Look at your dec page to see which endorsements or riders have been included with your policy.

- If you never look at another section of the insurance policy, DO REVIEW the "Claims" section because it tells you when and how to file a claim with the carrier. Your company will not be reimbursed for a covered loss if you fail to notify the carrier within the specified time limits.
- If you have time, look at the Exclusions section. After all, you don't want to waste time making a claim on a loss that is clearly not covered under the policy.
- If you're really ambitious, compare the Endorsements or Riders to the Terms and Conditions to track what has been deleted or revised. Make a note in the Terms and Conditions of what was changed by an Endorsement or Rider. It can be a backdoor way to exclude coverage for something you thought would be covered by the policy.

Insurance is divided into two broad categories: (1) Property & Casualty and (2) Accident & Health, which may include life insurance. The chart below shows some common types of policies in each category.

Property & Casualty (P&C) Policies	Accident & Health (A&H) Policies
Liability: Commercial general liability (CGL or premises liability) Professional liability: Medical malpractice Legal malpractice Errors & omissions (E&O) Directors & officers (D&O) Employment practices liability (EPL) Property Kidnap & Ransom Commercial auto (company vehicles) Personal auto Homeowners insurance Pet insurance	Individual health policies Group health plans (employer-sponsored or union-sponsored) "Ancillary" products: Dental Vision Short-term disability Long-term disability Group life insurance Specific disease ("cancer") policies

Fidelity & Surety (subset of P&C): Bank forms (Forms 14, 15, 24, 25) Property loss Theft/Robbery/Embezzlement Fidelity bond (i.e., employee dishonesty policy) Construction payment & performance bonds Miscellaneous bonds: Probate administrator bonds Bankruptcy trustee bonds Public notary bonds	Life (may be a separate category from A&H): Individual life insurance policies Annuities

Making a Claim on Your Policy

Your company will suffer a loss at some point in time. Losses can come from many directions. Your business could be robbed or an employee could steal company property. A manager could suddenly go crazy and say something highly inappropriate to a subordinate. The internet could crash in a cyberattack causing a financial loss when you are unable to do business as you wait for the internet to be restored.

After a loss occurs, your first phone call should be to your insurance agent or to the insurance company to report the loss. Many small business owners prefer calling their agent for help in identifying the correct insurance policy and then notifying the appropriate carrier. There's no point in filing a claim against the wrong policy. That wastes time.

The insurance company will assign the claim to a claims adjuster who will begin investigating the details of your claim. The claims adjuster will verify that the claim was timely filed with the carrier and that the loss *might be* covered by the policy. The claims adjuster will then investigate the details of the loss.

Here's the reality that often infuriates business owners. Your business suffered the loss but the insurance company wants you to stay out of the way unless you are specifically asked to participate. The claims adjuster will handle everything, including defending any lawsuits by third parties and settling the claim.

That can lead to another horrible fact about insurance claims. Most policies now include the "cost of defense" in the coverage limits. The cost of defense is sometimes referred to as the "burn layer" by insurance professionals. It's what you and your insurance company can expect to pay to defend against an injured party's claim against the company.

Imagine that your policy has a $1 million coverage limit and the insurance company spends $800,000 fighting a lawsuit related to the claim. After the defense costs, there will be only $200,000 in coverage limits remaining. As a result, any judgment or settlement exceeding $200,000 will be "excess loss" which is the responsibility of the company.

Example of "cost of defense" included in coverage limits

$ 1,000,000 policy coverage limit

- 800,000 cost to defend a lawsuit

$ 200,000 coverage limits remaining

- 300,000 judgment or settlement of lawsuit

$ <100,000> excess loss which must be paid by the insured

The moral of the story is that your company must periodically review your insurance coverage to ensure that the dollar limits are keeping up with your company's potential liabilities.

MITIGATION
OF RISKS

As you've seen throughout this book, there are plenty of risks to owning and running a small business. Of course, everything we do from the moment we're born carries risk. A life without risk would be bland and boring.

As a business owner, or HR manager or compliance officer, you want to manage your risks. The most common management tool is to mitigate risks through a good insurance program that covers key risks. The other most common tool is to create internal controls that allow problems to be caught before they can sink your business.

Unfortunately, the best insurance coverage or internal controls won't stop things from going wrong. When things go wrong, there are two actions that you must take to mitigate the risks you face.

First, stop digging a deeper hole. A bad situation can always be made worse by snap decisions based on emotional reactions in the immediate aftermath of the unfortunate event. Second, avoid the blame game. The goal is to figure out what went wrong so that the same mistake doesn't happen again.

Investigating What Happened

As the owner, or HR manager or compliance officer for your company, you will be called upon to lead or to assist in an investigation of what went wrong. Believe me: things will go wrong. Your involvement will be based on two assumptions: (1) you are a neutral observer because you are not personally involved in what went wrong; and (2) you will have to recommend revisions to existing compliance policies or create new policies to prevent the same problem in the future.

Below are two alternate methods for investigating what went wrong. Both alternatives will achieve the same goals of (1) fixing a current problem and (2) preventing (hopefully) the same problem from happening again. Any internal investigation needs to follow these general steps.

Informal investigation method

This informal method may be most useful when you are handling an on-going crisis, as happens frequently in HR matters. This method focuses on simultaneously (1) gathering information on what has already happened so that you can recommend how to fix the problem and (2) mitigating the company's liability while continuing to investigate the situation.

1. Create a list of the allegations. This will help define where to look for information.
2. Gather company records that might prove/disprove the allegations. For example, you might need to review payroll records, or CCTV video, or cell phones images and video or social media posts. You will also need a list of witnesses (co-workers, customers, vendors, etc.).
3. Create a chronological timeline based on the above records. This will help you when you're ready to take statements from the former employee and witnesses. People are imprecise in their recollections. They'll tell you about something that happened but not when. Plugging each witness's statement into the timeline can help clarify what happened.
4. Interview all witnesses to the event. During the interview, you'll want the witness to tell you only what she or he saw and heard. You will also need to caution the individual that all statements are expected to be confidential to ensure that the process is fair to all those involved.
5. Create a summary report that incorporates your review of the relevant company records, witness statements and other documentation involved in this investigation. The summary report should also include your recommendations of how to resolve the situation and (more importantly) prevent it from happening again. The final decision on how to proceed must be made by the senior management team, not by the HR manager or compliance officer.

Formal investigation method

A formal investigation method is a Root Cause Analysis and it will be familiar to anyone with a hard sciences or engineering background. This process is invaluable in situations that are complex with myriad possible sources of what went wrong.

This method is used to review a crisis that has already occurred and that needs to be analyzed to prevent a repetition of the crisis. The graphs and flow charts created during the investigation are invaluable in studying your company's operational procedures to spot the weak points and flaws in the process that were the direct cause of what went wrong. There are four major steps to this method.

1. Data collection. This step involves getting statements from eye witnesses, taking photos of the scene (if appropriate), looking at physical evidence and doing whatever is necessary to ascertain what happened and how it happened. Data collection will often continue through the next two steps of this process.

2. Causal factor charting. This step involves creating a graph or flow chart that tracks the sequence of events to identify what went wrong. The chart begins at a point just before the crisis occurred and then adds in all the data collected to track who did what and when at every point of the crisis. The chart ends at a point after the crisis has occurred. The purpose is to identify all actions that contributed to the crisis and thus could be root causes of the problem.

3. Root cause identification. In this step, the investigator identifies all the root causes using the information gathered in steps 1 and 2. The investigator often creates a flow chart to show the actions that contributed to the crisis and thus were root causes.

4. Recommendation generation and implementation. The investigator generates a report that summarizes the above steps and makes recommendations on how to avoid the same crisis in the future.

As you'll no doubt realize, Root Cause Analysis is much more involved than this brief synopsis indicates. It's used by engineers, after all. If you are interested in learning more about this method, there is a great deal of information readily available from a variety of sources.

> Root Cause Analysis is demonstrated in the TV documentary series, *Air Disasters* which follows real life investigations by the National Transportation Safety Board (NTSB) of plane crashes and near misses.
>
> Each program takes the viewer through the process used by the investigators to piece together the series of events leading up to the disaster or almost disaster. The show ends with a summary of the investigators' recommendations on safety upgrades to prevent similar mishaps in the future. In addition to learning about how Root Cause Analysis is done, you'll feel much safer about flying.
>
> A companion series is *Disasters at Sea*.

Regardless of which investigative method you use......remember that things will go wrong and crises will erupt. The inevitability of future crises is what makes HR and corporate compliance work both maddening and exhilarating. The only guarantee you have is that no crisis will ever be exactly the same!

Next Steps

After reading this book, you might be wondering why you ever wanted to start a company in the first place. Or you may be wondering whether you want to be an HR director or compliance officer. But fear not! Remember that you are an entrepreneur or a senior manager for your company because you have a unique set of skills set. Your skills may not be as unique as the skills of Liam Neeson in the *Taken* movies (we can't all be tall, Irish lads!) but your company needs your skills.

Every challenge you face can be resolved with a little help from your friends. Entire industries exist to help small business owners, from lawyers to CPA's, from social media marketers to IT support, from insurance agents to HR consultants. So build your network of business contacts and when you face a hurdle you can easily find someone to help you.

APPENDIX

STATUTES and REGULATIONS

Federal Laws

Abbreviations used in the chart of federal laws:

- CFR means the Code of Federal Regulations. Each time a new federal law is created, a regulatory agency responsible for implementing the new law must create rules. Those rules are called regulations and are collected in the CFR. The CFR is organized by title, parts and subparts, and sections. When you see a citation below, such as 29 CFR §2590.715-1251, it means the new regulation is codified in title 29 (Labor) at subpart 2590 (group health plans) in section 715-1251.
- Pub. Law. means Public Law, which is the format for a new federal law. Public Laws are usually a mashup of updates to existing laws and new laws which must then be incorporated into the existing titles and sections of the USC, in a process called "codification".
- USC means the United States Code, which contains all the federal laws organized into titles and sections by subject matter. When you see a citation below, such as 26 USC §6056, it means the new law is codified in title 26 (Taxation) at section 6056.

Name of the Law	Citation	Summary
Affordable Care Act or ACA (a/k/a ObamaCare) The ACA was actually enacted in two public laws: the Patient Protection and Afford-able Care Act (PPACA) and the Health Care and Education Reconciliation Act	Pub. Law 111-148 Pub. Law 111-152	The health care reform law is two separate laws that are collectively called the "Affordable Care Act". The law applies to all employers, (including churches and local governments who are exempt from ERISA). All regulations related to this law are jointly written and issued by the HHS, DOL, and IRS. (HHS regulations apply to insurers and aren't included here.)
ACA – large employer penalty	26 USC §4980H 26 CFR §54.4980H-1	Large employer penalty. The penalty was later reduced to $0, meaning that it no longer exists as practical matter.
ACA – large employer reporting requirement	26 USC §6056	Large employers must report to IRS on details of the group health plan offered to employees. Even though there is no longer an employer penalty, the report-ing requirement remains in effect.

Name of the Law	Citation	Summary
ACA – PCORI tax	26 USC §4376	PCORI tax paid by employers with self-funded health plans or HSA's. Due annually by July 31st.
ACA – "Cadillac tax"	26 USC §4980I	The "Cadillac tax" imposes a tax on group health plans with minimal or no deductibles, co-pays or coinsurance, such as plans for senior executives and their families or plans for unionized workers. The IRS has not finalized regulations yet.
ACA – Marketplace notice to employees	29 USC §218B DOL Technical Rel. 2013-02	Employers must notify employees of the Marketplace.
ACA – prohibited exclusions	29 CFR §2590.715-1251 to 29 CFR §2590.715-2719A	§2590.715-2704: pre-existing condition exclusion prohibited. §2590.715-2708: 90 days waiting period.

Name of the Law	Citation	Summary
Age Discrimination in Employment Act (ADEA)	29 USC §621, et seq. 29 CFR Parts 1625, 1626, and 1627	This law applies to all employers and is designed to protect employees aged 40 and older from age discrimination. Employers are required to post notices about this law (along with other employment laws) and must keep detailed records to prove they did not discriminate against older workers.
Americans with Disabilities Act (ADA) and the ADA Amendment Act (ADAAA)	42 USC § 12101, et seq. 29 CFR Parts 1630, 1640, and 641	This federal law applies to employers with 15 or more employees. It defines a disability is a "physical or mental impairment that substantially limits one or more major life activities". Under the ADAAA, if an employer treats an employee as disabled, the employee will be deemed to be disabled. Employers are prohibited from discriminating against an employee with a disability and are required to make reasonable accommodations to allow the disabled employee to perform the essential functions of the job unless doing so creates an undue hardship for the employer.

Name of the Law	Citation	Summary
Civil Rights Act of 1964 (Title VII)	42 USC §2000e 29 CFR Parts 1604 - 1608	This law prohibits employers with 15 or more employees from discriminating based on race, color, religion, national origin, or sex. Prohibits retaliating against a person who complains of discrimination. Also, employers must reasonably accommodate applicants' & employees' sincerely held religious practices, unless it would impose an undue hardship on business operations.
Consolidated Omnibus Budget Reconciliation Act (COBRA)	Pub. Law 99-272 Labor regulations: 29 CFR§2590.606-1 to 29 CFR §2590.606-4 Tax regulations: 26 CFR §54.4908B-2 to 26 CFR §54.4908B-10	This law applies to all employers with 20 or more employees. It allows employees and dependents of employees who participated in the group health plan to elect to continue receiving group health plan coverage after a "qualifying event" occurs. The most common "qualified event" is termination of employment, whether voluntarily or involuntarily. COBRA coverage is a minimum of 18 months and a maximum of 36 months if there is a disability.

Name of the Law	Citation	Summary
Consumer Credit Protection Act	15 USC §1671, et seq. 29 CFR Part 870	Title III of this law prohibits an employer from firing an employee whose wages are being garnished. The law sets a limit on the amount that may be garnished from each paycheck. It also allows garnishment for spousal or child support owed by the employee.
Controlling the Assault of Non-Solicited Pornography and Marketing Act (CAN-SPAM)	15 USC §103, et seq. 16 CFR Part 316	This law restricts sending unsolicited commercial messages to computers, cell phones, or fax machines. Please note that this is *not* limited to soliciting consumers; there is no exception for business-to-business solicitations. This law also requires that an unsolicited electronic message must be truthful and it must give information on how the recipient can opt out of future messages, by clicking on the "unsubscribe" link at the bottom of the email or blog. Each separate email is a violation subject to a penalty up to $16,000.

Name of the Law	Citation	Summary
Employment Retirement Income Security Act of 1974 (ERISA) – group health plans	29 USC §1001, et seq. Group health plan regulations: 29 CFR Part 2590	This 1974 law establishes employer responsibilities and employee rights related to retirement plans and group health plans. The definitions are in §1002. Part 2590 regulations cover group health plans.
Employment Retirement Income Security Act of 1974 (ERISA) – retirement plans	29 CFR Parts 2530 and 2550	Part 2530 sets the rules for pension plans. Part 2550 sets the fiduciary rules for pension plans.
Fair and Accurate Credit Transactions Act of 2003 (FACT Act or FACTA)	Pub L 108-159 16 CFR Part 602	This law amended the FCRA to create standards to prevent identity theft, improve the accuracy of information in consumer credit reports, and make it easier for consumers to obtain copies of their credit reports and to resolve disputes related to information included in their credit reports.

Name of the Law	Citation	Summary
Fair Credit Reporting Act (FCRA)	15 USC §1681, et seq. 16 CFR Part 604	This law applies to financial institutions (banks, credit unions, credit card issuers, and insurance companies), consumer credit reporting agencies, and employers who run credit checks on employees. A pre-employment background check of a job applicant's personal finances is a "credit check." The law sets out the requirements for reporting consumer credit information and how that information can be used by other creditors and employers. The credit reporting must relate to "credit or insurance used primarily for personal, family or household purposes."
Fair Debt Collections Practices Act	15 USC §1692 - §1692p 12 CFR Part 1006	This law sets guidelines for debt collection against consumers. It prohibits calling a person's workplace, threatening a debtor with jail for non-payment, threatening to sue when the creditor has no intention to file suit, and so on.

Name of the Law	Citation	Summary
Fair Labor Standards Act (FLSA)	29 USC §201, et. Seq. 29 CFR Parts 516, 531, 541 (partial listing)	This law sets the 40-hour work week and defines who are "exempt" or "non-exempt" employees. The overtime rules at 29 CFR Part 541 are currently under revision.
Fair Labor Standards Act (FLSA) - nursing mothers	29 USC §207(r)	Under, employers with more than 50 employees must allow an unpaid break for nursing mothers to express breast milk. This FLSA section was added by the ACA.
Family Medical Leave Act (FMLA)	29 USC §2601 - §2654 Labor regulations: 29 CFR Part 825 Tax regulations: 26 CFR §54.4980	This law applies to employers with a minimum of 50 employees working at one or more locations within 75 miles of each other. The law allows an employee to take up to 12 weeks of unpaid leave for the employee's medical condition, to care for a "family member" or for certain activities in connection with a family member's military service. It also allows up to 26 weeks of leave to care for a family member who acquired a serious health condition while on active duty in the armed services.

Name of the Law	Citation	Summary
Genetic Information Non-dis-crimination Act (GINA)	29 CFR Part 1635 See also HIPAA rule on this: 29 CFR §2590.702-1	This federal regulation prohibits employers from using the genetic information of an employee as the basis for employment decisions, such as hiring/firing an employee or whether to offer group health coverage to the employee.
Gramm-Leach-Bliley Act (GLB)	15 USC §6801 - §6809 16 CFR Part 313	This federal law applies to "financial institutions" (banks, credit unions, credit card issuers, insurance companies) that offer consumers financial products or services like loans, financial or investment advice and insurance. It limits sharing consumer financial information and protects a consumer's "non-public personal information."
HIPAA pro-hibition on pre-existing conditions and credit-ablecoverage	29 USC §2590.701-1 to §2590.701-6	These federal regulations relate to both COBRA and HIPAA rules limiting pre-ex-isting condition exclusions and the creditable coverage letter that shows an individ-ual had coverage during a specified time period and so should not be subjected to a pre-ex. Note that the ACA prohibits pre-existing condi-tion exclusions.

Name of the Law	Citation	Summary
HIPAA non-dis-crimination regulation	29 CFR §2590.702 to §2290.702-1	These regulations prohibit discrimination based on health factors such as health status, medical condition or disability and genetic infor-mation. Note that the rules on wellness programs are at §702(g). The ACA prohibits discrimination based on health factors.
HIPAA privacy and security	Pub. Law 104-191 45 CFR Parts 160 and 164	Part 160 sets out the require-ments of a group health plan (indirectly meaning the employer) to safeguard the "protected health information" (PHI) of each participant in the group health plan. Part 164 sets the standards for storing and transmitting electronic PHI. It also sets out detailed procedures for reporting a breach of security and the penalties for such a breach.

Name of the Law	Citation	Summary
National Labor Relations Act (NLRA)	29 USC §151 - §169 29 CFR Part 102 29 CFR §103.40 – joint employer definition	This law applies to all private sector employers regardless of the number of employees. Enacted in 1935, it was originally aimed at promoting better labor relations between unions and employers. In recent years the law has been expanded to protect non-union employees who engage in "concerted activity" related to employment conditions and pay.
Pregnancy Discrimination Act	42 USC §2000e 29 CFR Part 1604	This law applies to employers with at least 15 employees and prohibits discriminating against a woman because of pregnancy, childbirth or a medical condition related to pregnancy or childbirth. A Title VII law.
Providing Urgent Maternal Protections for Nursing Mothers Act (PUMP)	29 USC §218d	This law applies to employers with at least 50 employees. This 2023 law modifies the Fair Labor Standards Act to require additional breaks and a private space for employees who are still nursing an infant under 1 year old to pump breast milk.

Name of the Law	Citation	Summary
Sarbanes-Oxley Act of 2002 (SOX)	Public Law 107-204 15 USC 78j-1: audit requirements 15 USC §78m: annual reporting & financial controls requirements 17 CFR §240.10A-2: audit committee independence 17 CFR §240.13a-14 and 17 CFR §240.15d-14: certification by president, CEO & CFO 17 CFR §240.13a-15 and 17 CFR §15d-15: proof of internal controls over financial reporting	This law applies to publicly traded companies. It requires companies to have outside auditors and internal financial controls to prevent accounting fraud. Senior managers must certify in writing that the accounting is accurate, and they face up to 20 years in prison if they commit financial fraud. Privately owned companies look to this law for guidance on accounting best practices. Non-profits with $25M in revenue must comply with the SOX requirement of an independent audit.
Speak Out Act	42 USC §19401, et seq.	This 2022 law prohibits employers from suing to enforce a non-disclosure agreement related to sexual harassment claims when those claims arise after the NDA was signed.

Name of the Law	Citation	Summary
Statute of limitations, general	28 USC §2415	6 years for a contract claim; 3 years for a tort (personal injury) claim.
Statute of limitations, Income tax collections	26 USC §6502	10 years from the date of the assessment by the IRS that taxes are owed.
Stored Communications Act	18 USC §2701, et seq.	This law prohibits "any person or entity" that stores electronic communications, including emails, from voluntarily disclosing that information to third parties. This law was the basis for several recent lawsuits by employees alleging that employers snooped through personal emails of the employees that were automatically stored on the employers' servers.
Telemarketing and Consumer Fraud and Abuse Prevention Act	15 USC §6102 to §6108 16 CFR Part 310	This law set standards for telemarketing and also created the Do Not Call list.

Name of the Law	Citation	Summary
Telephone Consumer Protect Act	47 USC §227	This law places restrictions on businesses that use automated telephone systems to make unsolicited calls, commonly known as robo calls.
Uniformed Services Employment and Reemployment Rights Act (USERRA)	38 USC §4301, et seq.	This law applies to employers with at least 1 employee. It allows individuals who have been on extended military deployment to return to their jobs without their employee benefits, seniority, or pay being affected by the military service.
Worker Adjustment and Retraining Notification (WARN) Act	29 USC §2101 to §2109 20 CFR Part 639	Private sector employers with at least 100 employees must provide 60 calendar days advance notice to employees of plant closings or mass layoffs. But DOL has no enforcement authority if employers don't comply.
§401(k) retirement plans	26 USC §401 26 CFR §1.401-0 to §1.401-3 26 CFR §1.401(a)(4)	Subpart (k) establishes the 401(k) "defined contribution" retirement plans, which is the most common today.
§403(b) retirement plans	26 USC §403 26 CFR §1.403(b)-1 to §1.403(b)(11)	Subpart (b) establishes a retirement plan for senior management level employees.

Tennessee Laws

Abbreviations used in the Chart of Tennessee laws:

- **TCA** means Tennessee Code Annotated. The "annotated" version includes summaries of court opinions interpreting the statute and is only available by subscription from Lexis/Nexis. An unannotated version of Tennessee's statutes is available via a link on the Tennessee Secretary of State website. Tennessee's statutes are organized by title, chapter, and section. When you see the citation TCA §8-50-112, it means title 8, chapter 50, section 112.

Name of the Law	Citation	Summary
Ban the Box law	TCA §8-50-112	Bans TN state government from asking about criminal convictions in the initial screening phase of a job application unless the job is a "covered position," meaning federal or state law disqualifies convicted persons from serving in such jobs. Private sector employers can use it as a guide for their own hiring practices.
Breast Milk Expressing by Employees	TCA §50-1-305	This applies to all TN employers with at least 1 employee and requires an employer to provide unpaid break times for this purpose. Overlaps with TN Pregnant Workers Fairness Act.
Business Corporation Act	TCA §48-11-101, et seq.	Chapters 11 – 28 set out all the legal requirements of for-profit corporations.
Consumer Protection Act, Tennessee (TCPA)	TCA §47-18-101, et seq.	Protects consumers (any natural person) from fraudulent sales of goods, services, real estate and pretty much anything that is sold to a consumer. This law allows a consumer to collect treble damages if the unfair or deceptive act was done willfully or knowingly.

Name of the Law	Citation	Summary
Disability Act	TCA §8-50-103 and §8-50-104	TN employers with 8 or more employees are prohibited from discriminating against otherwise qualified job applicants based solely on a physical, mental or visual disability.
Drug Free Workplace Programs	TCA §50-9-101, et seq.	Any TN employer with 5 or more employees can create one of these programs. These programs can be used to drug test job applicants and current employees. Companies get a 5% discount on their workers comp insurance premiums, which is usually enough to cover the cost of implementing a drug-free program.
Employee Online Privacy Act	TCA §50-1-1001, et seq.	Employers with at least 1 employee can't require job applicants or employees to provide passwords for personal internet accounts. But employers can ask for passwords for any company-provided electronic device (phone, iPad, etc.) in order to access the device for valid business reasons.

Name of the Law	Citation	Summary
Employing non-citizens	TCA §50-1-103 TCA §50-1-106	These laws prohibit TN employers from knowingly hiring illegal aliens and from using a federal individual tax identification number (TIN) to prove a person's immigration status.
Employment Security Law	TCA §50-7-101, et seq.	TN's unemployment compensation law. The key thing to remember is that even employees fired for cause will probably be able to collect unemployment. Look at §302 for the specific eligibility rules.
For-Profit Benefit Corporation Act	TCA §48-28-101, et seq	This is a relatively new type of for-profit corporate entity (a/k/a social enterprise corporation) that uses its profits to support artistic, charitable, cultural, economic, educational, environmental, literary, medical, religious, scientific or technological purposes.
"GLB" provisions in TN	TCA §56-8-119	This law mirrors the federal law but adds a Tennessee twist: *insurance agencies* are also required to protect "non-public personal information" as that phrase is defined under GLB.

Name of the Law	Citation	Summary
"Guns in parking lots" law	TCA §39-17-1313 TCA §50-1-312	Allows gun owners with permits to bring their guns to work as long as the guns are locked in the gun owner's car and out of sight. Employers are protected from civil liability if the guns are used. Employers can't fire an employee solely because the employee brings a gun to work as allowed by §39-17-1313.
Health Carrier Grievance & External Review Procedure Act	TCA §56-61-101, et seq.	TN law that implements the ACA requirement to create an appeal process for any person who is denied coverage on a claim.
Human Rights Act, Tennessee	TCA §4-21-101, et seq.	TN version of the federal anti-discrimination laws; applies to employers with 8 or more employees.

Name of the Law	Citation	Summary
Lawful Employment Act ("e-Verify" law)	TCA §50-1-701, et seq.	TN employers with 35 or more employees must use the e-Verify system to verify that new hires can legally work in the U.S. The portal is www.e-verify.gov. Employers with less than 35 employees are encouraged to use the e-Verify system. This state law doesn't replace the federal law requirement to complete a Form I-9 on new hires.
Non-Dis-closure Agreement prohibitions	TCA §50-1-108	Prohibits employers from including sexual harassment claims in a non-disclosure agreement to be signed by a current or prospective employee.
Non-profit Corporation Act	TCA §48-51-101, et seq.	Chapter 51 sets out the legal requirements for non-profit corporations.

Name of the Law	Citation	Summary
"Parental leave" act	TCA §4-21-408	This TN law applies to employers with 100 or more employees. It allows an employee to take up to 16 weeks of unpaid leave for the birth or adoption of a child. If both parents are state employees, the aggregate sick leave they may use is 30 days. Employers generally require this 16-week leave to run concurrent with FMLA leave.
Personal Rights Protection Act	TCA §47-25-1101, et seq.	A business must obtain an individual's consent to use the person's image (photo, video, etc.) for advertising or marketing purposes. This law exempts images gathered at news or sporting events.

Name of the Law	Citation	Summary
Plant Closings and Reduction in Operations	TCA §50-1-601, et seq.	This law applies to TN employers with 50 – 99 full-time employees at a workplace. The employer must notify the employees and the TN Dept. of Labor & Workforce Development if the workplace will be closed permanently or for a 3-month period. Similar federal law (the WARN Act) applies to companies with 100 or more employees.
Pregnant Workers Fairness Act	TCA §50-10-101 to §104	This TN law applies to employers with 15 or more employees. Employers must make a reasonable accommodation for workers who are pregnant or are nursing newborns. This might mean light duty, modified work schedules, privacy for breast milk expressing.
Private Pension and Retirement Plans	TCA §50-1-401	This law applies to any TN retirement plan not covered by ERISA. (This usually means local government or quasi-governmental entities.) It requires a separate trust account for employee contributions.

Name of the Law	Citation	Summary
Public Protection Act (Whistleblower protection)	TCA §50-1-304 TCA §50-1-310 (applies specifically to teachers)	The TN law applies to all employers with a minimum of 1 employee. As amended in 2014, an employee suing for retaliatory discharge must prove that the "sole reason" for being fired was the employee's refusal to participate in illegal activities (criminal law violations). Also, if a court decides the suit is frivolous, the employee can be assessed the court costs & legal fees of the employer. NOTE: 2021 amendment says that non-compliance with anti-discrimination laws isn't "illegal activities."
Reentry Success Act (Occupational licenses)	TCA §62-76-104	A prior criminal conviction can't be used as the basis to deny the individual an occupational license, unless the conviction directly relates to that occupation, profession, business or trade.
Reentry Success Act (Negligent hiring)	TCA §40-29-109	An employer can't be sued for negligent hiring or supervision based solely on the employee having a prior criminal conviction.

Name of the Law	Citation	Summary
Restoration of Citizenship	TCA §40-29-107	Employers may be protected from claims of negligent hiring or supervision when they hire employees with prior criminal conviction(s) who have obtained a "certificate of employability" from a court in the county where the person resides or where the crime occurred.
"State continuation" law (aka "mini-COBRA")	TCA §56-7-2312	This law applies to TN employers with 20 or fewer employees. The coverage is for a maximum of 3 months.
Statutes of limitations, Tennessee (This is a selective list)	TCA §28-3-104 TCA §28-3-105 TCA §28-3-109	Personal injury: 1 year from date of injury. Property damage: 3 years. Contract actions not specifically covered by other statutes: 6 years.
Uniform Partnership Act, Revised	TCA §61-1-101, et seq.	There are several different types of partnerships and each type has its own requirements.
Uniform Limited Partnership Act, Revised	TCA §61-2-101, et seq.	There are several different types of partnerships and each type has its own requirements.

Name of the Law	Citation	Summary
Uniform Limited Partnership Act of 2017	TCA §61-3-101, et seq.	There are several different types of partnerships and each type has its own requirements.
Wage Reporting in TN	TCA 50-7-404(c)(3)	Effective January 1, 2019, every employer must begin filing a quarterly Premium and Wage Report (Form LB-0441) with the Dept. of Labor & Workforce Development.
Workers Compensation laws	TCA §50-6-101, et seq.	These laws apply to any employer with a minimum of 5 employees. The laws set out detailed procedures on how to handle a workplace injury. Disputes related to injuries incurred after 7/1/2014 must be submitted to special workers compensation courts; TN courts no longer have jurisdiction on these cases. NOTE: 2021 amendment to §226 increases penalties on employers who fail to timely file WC claim or to pay claims.

Federal Regulatory Authorities

Name	Web Address	Comments
Department of Labor (DOL)	www.employer.gov	DOL website with compliance resources for employers. It includes compliance information for federal government contractors.
Department of Labor, Employee Benefits Security Administration (EBSA)	www.dol.gov/ebsa	EBSA interprets and enforces ERISA and all the laws incorporated into it.
Department of Labor, Wage and Hour Division (WHD)	www.dol.gov/whd	WHD enforces the rules on the Fair Labor Standards Act (FLSA), including non-exempt and exempt employees and overtime rules. It also enforces the Family Medical Leave Act (FMLA). The website includes FMLA model forms that are periodically updated by DOL. Using the forms means an employer has met the minimum legal requirements for complying with FMLA.

Name	Web Address	Comments
Equal Employment Opportunity Commission (EEOC)	www.eeoc.gov	This federal agency investigates employment discrimination allegations. The EEOC can sue an employer for violations of the law.
Federal Trade Commission	www.ftc.gov	Federal regulator of consumer protection laws. It also has oversight of debt collections by companies other than non-financial services institutions. If your company runs credit checks on job applicants, it is subject to FTC jurisdiction for any violations of the FCRA.
Health & Human Services (HHS)	www.hhs.gov	Enforces HIPAA privacy rules on protecting "personal health information" (PHI). It also enforces the security rule setting standards to protect PHI from database breaches.
Internal Revenue Service	www.irs.gov	Need we to explain who these guys are? Of course not! Corporations file federal income tax reports with the IRS annually.

Name	Web Address	Comments
National Labor Relations Board (NLRB)	www.nlrb.gov	Created in 1935 to protect the "concerted activity" of employees related to wages and working conditions. It now investigates union and non-union employee issues.
Securities and Exchange Commission (SEC)	www.sec.gov	Federal regulator of publicly-traded companies.
U.S. Customs & Immigration Service	www.uscis.gov www.e-verify.gov	This federal agency administers the e-Verify program and the Form I-9 requirement for new hires.

Tennessee Regulatory Authorities

Name	Web Address	Comments
Attorney General's Office	http://tn.gov/ attorneygeneral	Consumer complaints are filed with and investigated by this office. If the consumer complaint involves cyber-attacks, the business must notify the FBI to report the crime.

Name	Web Address	Comments
Human Rights Commission (THRC)	www.tn.gov/ humanrights/	The TN state version of the EEOC which has concurrent jurisdiction to investigate allegations of discrimination.
Department of Labor & Workforce Development	www.tn.gov/ workforce	Companies with employees must file a quarterly Premium & Wage Report via the links at the Labor Dept. website.
Department of Revenue (DOR)	www.tennessee. gov/revenue	New businesses must register with DOR by creating a tax account for the business.

Companies with Tennessee revenue must also file tax reports, such as the Franchise & Excise Tax or Sales & Use Tax, annually with the TN authorities. |

Name	Web Address	Comments
Secretary of State website	www.tennessee.gov/sos	Businesses must register with the SOS by filing a copy of their Articles of Incorporation (or the equivalent that is appropriate for their business type). Businesses also must file an Annual Report. This site has a wealth of information and links to resources for new businesses.

Useful Websites

Name	Web Address	Comments
Code of Federal Regulations (CFR)	www.ecfr.gov	This is where federal regulations are published after they become final. The regulations contain the details of how each federal agency enforces the federal laws within its scope of authority.
Federal Register (FR)	www.regula-tions.com	All proposed new federal regulations are published in the FR for a "notice and comment" period before being finalized. The final versions are also published in the FR.
Tennessee General Assembly (legislature)	www.legis-lature.state.tn.us	Track bills through the Senate and House to see what changes may be coming in state law. This site has plenty of useful information although it's not very user-friendly.

Additional Resources

This is a non-inclusive list of books that I have found helpful with my own business.

Built to Last, by Jim C. Collins (*This book was written before Good to Great but should be read after that book.*)

Built to Sell, by John Warrillow (A *quick, easy read explaining how to focus your business's product/service into a marketable and profitable enterprise.*)

Drive, by Daniel H. Pink (*Entertaining quick read about what motivates workers: money v. autonomy.*)

Good to Great, by Jim C. Collins (*The classic account of why some businesses continue to grow while others fail; learn about the "hedgehog" and "BHAG's".*)

How to Win Friends and Influence People, by Dale Carnegie (*Decades old but still the classic on how to treat others.*)

Profit First, by Mike Michalowicz (*A new approach to profit and loss statements and budgeting for non-accountants who are not good with math.*)

The 7 Habits of Highly Effective People, by Stephen R. Covey (*Another classic on building a successful business.*)

Start with Why, by Simon Sinek (*Identify the purpose for your business. Why does your business exist?*)

Think and Grow Rich, by Napoleon Hill (*Attitude affects outcomes.*)

Traction, by Gino Wickham (*The author is not a gifted writer but persevere. This book provides a step-by-step process for setting up, assigning responsibilities, and growing a business.*)

Acknowledgements

Thanks to my wonderful editor, Kate Stephenson, for cleaning up the manuscript of this book. Any remaining grammatical errors or other lapses are entirely my fault.

I am also grateful to the entire team at Epiphany Creative Services for once again guiding me through the world of self-publishing.

About the Author

Norma Shirk is an author, speaker, business owner and an attorney. She is founder and CEO of Corporate Compliance Risk Advisor LLC (CCRA), a human resources consulting firm for small to mid-size employers. She also helps employers assess their corporate risks in order to mitigate those risks through internal controls and insurance coverage. She is also a Certified Franchise Advisor (CFA) with Collaborative Franchise Systems (CFS), founded by Dr. Robert Needham. CFS assists business owners looking to franchise their model and sell franchise units as a strategy for building wealth. Ms. Shirk's contribution to the team effort draws upon her experience as a lawyer, human resources consultant, and business owner to help owners as they transition to franchisors.

Ms. Shirk earned a J.D. from the University of Tennessee-Knoxville School of Law and a B.A. (History) from Middle Tennessee State University. She holds law licenses in Tennessee, Texas, and Colorado.

With 20 years of experience, primarily in banking and insurance law, working with a variety of employers, in government and private industry, she has functioned in every role from a worker bee to a General Counsel. Her first book, *Psycho Bosses and Obnoxious Co-Workers*, takes an amusing look at workplace behavior and is available wherever fine books are sold. She resides in Nashville. www.complianceriskadvisor.com

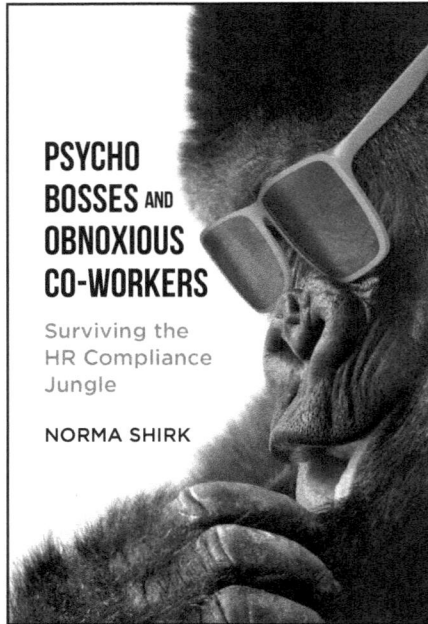

PSYCHO BOSSES and OBNOXIOUS CO-WORKERS

Surviving the HR Compliance Jungle

Are you working in the cubicle next to a slob? Or dealing with a boss that everyone, except senior management, knows is deranged? With bosses and coworkers like this, the workplace can be a jungle!

Human Resources professionals and company owners beat their way through the compliance foliage and undergrowth on any given day. For all of you who suffer, know that you're not alone! Take a ride through the funny side of workplaces. It's like a safari without the real animals—just the ones in your office. For all of you who suffer, know that you're not alone!

Ebook - ISBN: 978-1-7324885-0-2

Paperback - ISBN: 978-1-7324885-1-9

www.ingramcontent.com/pod-product-compliance
Lightning Source LLC
Chambersburg PA
CBHW040851210326
41597CB00029B/4798